HIGH-STAKES
TEACHING

HIGH-STAKES TEACHING

Practices That Improve Student Learning

Edited by
Terri Hebert
Sherry Durham

Rowman & Littlefield Education
Lanham • New York • Toronto • Plymouth, UK

Published in the United States of America
by Rowman & Littlefield Education
A Division of Rowman & Littlefield Publishers, Inc.
A wholly owned subsidiary of The Rowman & Littlefield Publishing Group, Inc.
4501 Forbes Boulevard, Suite 200, Lanham, Maryland 20706
www.rowmaneducation.com

Estover Road
Plymouth PL6 7PY
United Kingdom

Copyright © 2008 by Terri Hebert and Sherry Durham

All rights reserved. No part of this publication may be reproduced, stored in a retrieval system, or transmitted in any form or by any means, electronic, mechanical, photocopying, recording, or otherwise, without the prior permission of the publisher.

British Library Cataloguing in Publication Information Available

Library of Congress Cataloging-in-Publication Data
High-stakes teaching : practices that improve student learning / edited by Terri Hebert, Sherry Durham.
   p. cm.
Includes bibliographical references.
ISBN-13: 978-1-57886-880-3 (cloth : alk. paper)
ISBN-10: 1-57886-880-7 (cloth : alk. paper)
ISBN-13: 978-1-57886-881-0 (pbk. : alk. paper)
ISBN-10: 1-57886-881-5 (pbk. : alk. paper)
eISBN-13: 978-1-57886-922-0
eISBN-10: 1-57886-922-6
[etc.]
 1. Effective teaching. 2. Teacher–student relationships. 3. Academic achievement. I. Hebert, Terri. II. Durham, Sherry.
 LB1025.3.H54 2008
 371.102–dc22   2008025961

∞™ The paper used in this publication meets the minimum requirements of American National Standard for Information Sciences—Permanence of Paper for Printed Library Materials, ANSI/NISO Z39.48-1992.
Manufactured in the United States of America.

To my children,
John and Sarah,
who continue to teach me much about love, life, and learning.

—Terri Hebert

To my daughter and friend, Stephanie Ann.
You exemplify a love for learning and humanity that makes me very proud to be your mother.

—Sherry Durham

CONTENTS

Foreword ix
    Debbie Silver

Introduction xi

1 The Link Between Student Achievement and
   Caring Teachers   1
   Terri Hebert

2 A Gem in the Making   13
   Ann Guilbert

3 Caring in an Age of Accountability   23
   Nelda Wellman

4 The Transformative Power of Relationships   33
   Wendell Wellman

5 Do What They Say, Say What They Mean: One Thing
   Leads to Another   43
   Sherry Durham

6	The Impact of a Single Life *Terri Hebert*	53
7	The Science of Learning *Ann Guilbert*	67
8	When All Is Said and Done *Sherry Durham*	79
9	RIF: Reduction in Force or Realization in the Future *Terri Hebert*	89
10	Opportunity in the Face of Failure *Sherry Durham*	103
11	The Choices We Make *Terri Hebert and Sherry Durham*	111

FOREWORD

In a time when politically correct, quantifiable, expedient assessment of our schools' educational success is taking the forefront across America, it is important for the voice of the "other part" of education to be heard. If we are in fact going to hold ourselves truly accountable for the next generation and beyond, then perhaps we should ensure that we pay attention not only to cognitive standards but also to the promises set forth in most schools' mission statements—to promote lifelong learners who become creative, caring, contributing members of society. *High-Stakes Teaching: Practices That Improve Student Learning* offers a passionate, reasoned response to the nation's growing obsession with standardization; it gives vital research that backs up the premise "It's not just about the test scores." The authors use current thinking from educational experts to validate the idea that the *art* of teaching is most effective when fused with the *heart* of teaching. They weave their important line of reasoning through realistic stories and examples.

Talk to any educator in the field, and you will hear countless anecdotes about how student lives were changed forever by an event, a kindness, or a challenge that was offered by a teacher.

Readers can probably list their own recollections of teachers who profoundly affected their lives. These life-changing experiences are not easily measured nor standardized. This book takes a critical look at the importance of supporting teachers in their efforts to leave an indelible mark on the future via their impact on young souls.

Debbie Silver, teacher and author of
Drumming to the Beat of Different Marchers

INTRODUCTION

On the evening of October 4, 1957, Americans tuned in as an NBC radio network reporter announced to the audience, "Listen now for the sound that forevermore separates the old from the new." As his words reverberated through the radio transmitters, men and women, boys and girls heard for the first time a strange and unusual chirping sound emanating from space. The beeps, heard in the key of A-flat, lasted for just a second, were followed by a brief pause, and then continued again in a steady rhythmic pattern until the object had passed out of range. The satellite, known as Sputnik, was relatively small—about the size of a beach ball, weighing 184 pounds; yet the impact of its presence was enormous.

Since that autumn day, Americans have witnessed headline after headline swell and then retreat much like the evening tide. Only a few have stood out long enough to cause its citizens to question foundational beliefs, though when this does occur, the gut-wrenching and painful images associated with such an event typically strike a chord inside each of us, inviting us to enter into deep reflection. It is at this moment that Americans ask the hard questions and diligently seek honest answers.

This was how it was on October 5, 1957—the day after our country heard Sputnik's sound—and continued for several years later. A growing number of educators sensed the need to improve upon the status quo, yet little was actually done until the starter gun sounded the beginning of the space race. Our nation's sense of national security had been threatened, and this served as a catalyst for the U.S. Congress to step in and provide funding for the development of innovative and hands-on curricula with the sole purpose of catching up with the Russians (Eisner 1992). During the 1960s, approximately $100 million was spent on the reeducation of teachers, shifting the learning experience from lecture-driven to hands-on methods. By the 1970s, the United States had reclaimed its place in the scientific world, as Americans walked on the moon's surface and the job market reverberated the need for engineers, scientists, and technicians (Kubota 1997).

As one reflects upon today's educational system, little evidence of the shift from lecture to higher-order engagement within the classroom remains. We now are seeing an emphasis of high-stakes testing programs emerge, with formula-based requirements on reading, math, and writing—the latest of which is named *No Child Left Behind*—dictating to teachers the methodology used and disregarding their expertise and autonomy within the classroom.

Because of the heightened level of accountability being placed on students, teachers, and administrators, stress levels have continued to increase. Teachers are devoting larger blocks of time and resources in the preparation of their students for standardized tests, as they fear the repercussions coming from concerned groups (Jorgenson & Vanosdall 2002). In the frenzy to prepare students for the tests, many teachers simply forget the basics: care, hope, and love. You might ask yourself, "How can one person forget to care for those in the classroom? How can one forget to love one another? How can one misplace hope?" But as time continues to be eaten up by test preparation and then testing, there is very little time to actually get to know those who are within your care, especially as you enter the middle and high school grades.

High-Stakes Teaching: Practices That Improve Student Learning touches on those individuals who are currently teaching in U.S. public schools. They are realizing that to effectively reach all students, one must begin with a sense of care and hope about those seated at the desks.

Sherry Durham is adjunct professor in the Department of Curriculum and Instruction for Sam Houston State University located in Huntsville, Texas. She is also associate director of special education for the Lufkin Independent School District in Lufkin, Texas.

Terri Hebert is assistant professor within the University of Central Arkansas's College of Education's Department of Teaching, Learning, and Technology and program coordinator of the Advanced Studies in Teaching and Learning, a master's in education program. The university is located in Conway, Arkansas.

Nelda Wellman and Wendell Wellman, a husband-and-wife team, are serving Northwestern State University's College of Education as assistant professors. Their location is in Natchitoches, Louisiana.

Ann Guilbert is the K–12 science coordinator and academic dean of the Sylvan Hills Feeder Pattern for Pulaski County Special School District, which is located in Little Rock, Arkansas.

In Chapter 1, "The Link Between Student Achievement and Caring Teachers," Terri Hebert explores the lives of two teachers who exemplified caring traits toward their students while also exhibiting hope for the future. The impact of Mrs. Calvin and Marisol upon the lives of children continues to reverberate even today and quietly invites each member of the profession to examine their own classroom for such characteristics.

In Chapter 2, "A Gem in the Making," Ann Guilbert describes three educators who set lofty goals for themselves and their students and whose actions exhibit a deep concern for all students as they meet the level of expectation required for today's success.

In Chapter 3, "Caring in an Age of Accountability," Nelda Wellman discusses the opportunities found within writing—to gain a deeper understanding of the students as well as allowing the students an opportunity to get to know themselves. Often, many of our students do not take the time to reflect on internal feelings and emotions. By doing so, ideas and areas of conflict can be synthesized in an attempt at purification.

In Chapter 4, "The Transformative Power of Relationships," Wendell Wellman presents the story of a counselor and two of his students as they each find meaning in the other. Oftentimes we find that the courage to do what is right proves difficult, but even in the midst of despair, hope can be seen.

In Chapter 5, "Do What They Say, Say What They Mean: One Thing Leads to Another," Sherry Durham examines an assistant principal assigned to a bilingual elementary campus and her ability to maintain campus discipline. This sounds like a fairly simple charge, but sometimes the lessons learned are more meaningful to the adult involved rather than the student. This is the case with Arlene.

In Chapter 6, "The Impact of a Single Life," Terri Hebert blends the two worlds of Mark and Nancy as they seek to find innovative ways to reach out to a racially and economically divided world. Both educators exhibit a strong determination to combine the "virtue of a clear goal . . . and the flexibility of . . . clever and distinct strategies" (Gould 2003, p. 276), moving the entire classroom from Point A to Point B, from the beginning to the end of the learning experience.

In Chapter 7, "The Science of Learning," Ann Guilbert reflects on the changes within a science classroom, moving the reader from the traditional to the constructivist approach. She shares the story of Meredith, a teacher who unleashed her students' curiosity through such an approach while balancing discovery and creativity within a test-driven world.

In Chapter 8, "When All Is Said and Done," Sherry Durham examines the impact one teacher can have on the life of a student. As Carol began the school year with more frustration than previous years, she wondered if retirement was the answer. Instead of walking away, she walked into one student's life. Instead of focusing merely on the instructional outcome of her class, she focused on the journey.

In Chapter 9, "RIF: Reduction in Force or Realization in the Future," Terri Hebert reflects on a current trend in many school districts as they attempt to streamline jobs and budgets. The story is told through the eyes of one administrator who was part of the reduction in force. Through the entire process, she witnessed a personal truth in the adage, "when one door closes, another one opens."

In Chapter 10, "Opportunity in the Face of Failure," Sherry Durham shares the story of Wilson, a teacher who came into the profession after many years spent in the financial industry. During Wilson's short tenure at Valley View Elementary, he realized his calling in the profession and found himself quite happy teaching science to fifth graders. However, with the hiring of a new principal and the shift in the school's vision, a storm was brewing in Wilson's path. He held tight to his calling and found opportunity, even in the face of failure.

Chapter 11, "The Choices We Make," serves as the book's conclusion. Terri Hebert and Sherry Durham summarize the writing by challenging the reader to examine educational choices that are made in an effort to visualize the impact upon those around us—our students, their parents, and the community—as well as the personal impact on the one making the choice, the educator. It must be the goal of education to purposefully make choices that will encourage and extend the learning experiences of our students because all too soon our students will be adults facing choices of their own.

REFERENCES

Eisner, E. W. (1992). Educational reform and the ecology of schooling. *Teachers College Record*, 93(4), 610–627.

Gould, S. J. (2003). *The hedgehog, the fox, and the magister's pox: Ending the false war between science and humanities*. New York: Harmony.

Jorgenson, O., & Vanosdall, R. (2002). High-stakes testing: The death of science? What we risk in our rush toward standardized testing and the three R's. *Phi Delta Kappan, 83*(8), 601–612.

Kubota, C. (1997). Preparation and professional development of K–12 science teachers in the United States. *Peabody Journal of Education, 72*(1), 129–149.

THE LINK BETWEEN STUDENT ACHIEVEMENT AND CARING TEACHERS

Terri Hebert

One must care about a world one will never see.

—Bertrand Russell

The focus of today's educators revolves around testing issues and the outcomes that will be produced by their students. As the stakes continue to be ratcheted up by administrators, education boards, and policymakers, large percentages of children feel less and less cared for and attended to while in the classroom (Lawrence, Jones, & Smith 1999). However, teachers who still find a way to develop an attitude of care toward their students also have found that even amid rigorous testing measures, hope can spring forth like a well in a dry and parched land.

Even though Beth was only 5 years old, she vividly remembers her introduction to public schooling and the excitement that her mother and grandmother exhibited in the days leading up to her enrollment. It was fun to shop for a new dress and shoes and a lunchbox complete with a metal Thermos. However, the actual experience, in her opinion, was found lacking and failed to produce any thrills. Beth was not ready to leave her family and everything familiar, even for just a few short hours each day. It seemed that as the group representing three generations walked toward the entrance of that one-room, red schoolhouse where the kindergarten teacher stood to greet each child, Beth became more and more uncomfortable.

The building was located in the teacher's backyard and was surrounded by a white picket fence and an overabundance of massive, hardwood trees. As mother, grandmother, and Beth approached the door of the little red schoolhouse, Beth's muscles began to contract, forcing her grip on her mother's hand to tighten. Eventually though, after some coaxing, the small hand left the safety of her mother's and reached out for the unknown hand of her teacher. Mrs. Calvin tenderly led the small and timid girl into the classroom and introduced her to the other children. She assigned a desk and a handwriting book to Beth, as she did with each new student. Before the school day ended, and to Beth's surprise, she had fallen in love with the classroom and with Mrs. Calvin. She had fallen in love with learning.

During the early years of American schools, there were no achievement tests. Children were not required to take kindergarten entrance exams. In fact, kindergarten was not even a required grade, and there were no tests to determine whether youngsters were ready to be promoted. Each child simply and joyfully learned. However, the lessons exceeded anything that could have ever been captured on paper, dealing with matters of heart, soul, and mind. Children inquisitively observed the beauty found in their artistic renderings; each person participated joyfully in the creation of his or her own music while skillfully mastering the language of school. In the presence of caring teachers, children were allowed to blossom and grow into individuals of worth.

Times have certainly changed. No longer is there the relaxed atmosphere found in these earlier years, when children were praised for creativity and innovation. Now teachers can be observed frantically preparing their students for yet another test. Time for exploring nuances of music, art, and literature has been swallowed up with drills and practice of disembodied facts, letters, and numbers. Writing as a means to capture thoughts and dreams has been replaced with simplistic formulas. One 5th-grade teacher illustrates such a formula with her comment on the writing portion of the state test:

> All of a sudden the wording of the test changes and people are thrown for a loop. As they announce the changes, people just start sighing. I remember in one of those training workshops, a lady sitting near me griped and griped that there were now sixteen lines on the box for the open response instead of twelve. I asked how her teaching would have changed if she had known that information ahead of time, and she matter-of-factly said that she would've taught the children how to write using sixteen lines instead of twelve.

Learning for the sake of learning has been traded in for a newer model: learning for the sake of passing a test.

TIME TO REFLECT

Think back to your introduction to schooling. What do you remember about the initial experience? Are your memories of learning positive or negative? Describe them, and as you do, think about the role high-stakes testing played during that time.

HOPE AND CARE IN TODAY'S CLASSROOM

In 2001, President Bush signed into law the No Child Left Behind (NCLB) Act, which promised to advance the culture of American education through tougher standards and testing. The original construct of NCLB struck a chord with Americans about equality in education. We as a nation believe that all children should have the right to a free and equal schooling experience, however the end results have been rather disappointing, only providing an increase in the quantity of tests without necessarily advancing a child's quality of learning. Beck (1994) sums this up: "Universal rights, handed to people whether or not they seek them, cannot compensate for losses of identity, group respect, and community feeling" (p. 12).

Problems continue to develop as students, teachers, and administrators feel the pressure to perform at ever-increasing levels. The rising stress accounts for a growing number of teachers and students simply giving up. Educators choose to leave the profession at an earlier age, or they request a grade change to where the tests are not given. Young people are opting for a grade-equivalent diploma instead of completing their high school career. Little value has been gained among student subpopulations, forcing them to attempt to either perform on a higher grade level than they are capable of or read in a language other than their native tongue.

Concerns by administrators have increased about the lack of innovation and creativity found within classrooms, especially during walk-through evaluations. In spite of this, mandates from state departments of education continue to be written about the need to streamline curricular choices, to provide more and more benchmarking exams, and to cut extracurricular activities from the school day (Corbett & Wilson 1991; Smith 1991; Firestone, Mayrowetz, & Fairman 1998).

One must ask: Where has the joy and passion of the craft gone? Where are the teachers, like Mrs. Calvin, who truly care for and instill within their students a love of learning? Noddings (1992), a Stanford University professor of educational philosophy, believes that "schools should be committed to a great moral purpose: to care for children so that they, too, will be prepared to care" (p. 65). This care in classrooms does not necessarily mean stickers on papers expressing "warm fuzzies" and smiley faces; rather, "care implies a continuous search for competence and includes fostering in students the knowledge and skills necessary to make a positive contribution in whatever field of study or work they might choose" (Oakes & Lipton 1999, p. 251). The impending failure of NCLB will occur not because of its bureaucratic complexity or its costly demands on society but because of its inability to reach the whole person, the child and the teacher, in an attempt to create a relational school.

Vygotsky (1978) and other socioculturalists validate that learning takes place in and through caring relationships and that social and cognitive development are inseparably bound together. The classroom should resemble a community of searchers each looking for what is and is not known: the teacher searching for learning evidence provided by the student and the student searching for his and her own discovery. Naturally, this type of environment might appear unruly to an outsider, yet the ebb and flow of noise and movement as learners present their ideas, investigate possibilities, and reach conclusions are sweet sounds to a trained educator's ear.

Hope rises each time a learner searches for an answer. Care presented by the instructor encourages the process as it unfolds. The relationships between teacher and student shape multiple facets of learning, expressly found within the academic, intrapersonal, institutional, and cultural settings. As Bruner (1996) confirms, "Learning, remembering, talking, imagining: all of them are made possible by participating in a culture" (p. xi), "so, in the end, while mind creates culture, culture also creates mind" (p. 166).

> **TIME TO REFLECT**
>
> What does a caring classroom look like to you? Do you believe that a caring classroom is necessary for student success? Have you been a part of a community of searchers? If so, what role did you play?

HOPE FREES THE SPIRIT AND CHALLENGES THE MIND

As Sherry approached the door of her classroom, she noticed a much younger woman than was expected, with two long, flowing braids of rich, brown hair. Marisol teaches 2nd-grade bilingual children, many of whom are new to the United States and have not yet fully grasped the language. She unashamedly shares her love of quilting with her students and with Sherry, as all watch her skillful placement of cloth remnants onto a larger cotton piece. Marisol talks as she continues to work. It is her goal, just as the quilt has become one through the stitching together of many pieces, to bring about this oneness in the classroom even though there are many cultures and beliefs represented.

When asked who was most influential to Marisol on her educational journey as a child, she immediately reflects first upon the role of her parents and then her 4th-grade teacher. She begins by talking about her mother:

> She does not have an education. She [only] went to second grade in Mexico and that was as far as she got. But whatever she learned in school and throughout life, she tried her best to pass it on . . . you know as far as mathematics or working hard. She couldn't help me with any of my homework other than basic math, but she gave me the space to do my work and required that it be done correctly. I was very fortunate that she was a stay-at-home mom. Yet because of her decision to remain with me at home, our family was considered to be poor. I did not know we were poor. I thought that was what every mom did—stay at home and help their children with school.

Marisol continues with her thoughts on the role her father played in her education, although she maintains mixed feelings about him. His provision of a home, along with granting Marisol permission to obtain an education, offered her the grounding that was needed. Her father once said that she was honored as a "person and a female." Those words encouraged her to go beyond the traditional role of a Hispanic woman and seek something more from life:

> A lot of my barrio girlfriends and their parents didn't see education as important for females in the family. They were just going to grow up, have a bunch of children, and be ordered around by some man. Why did they need an education to do that? It was looked down

upon if the women were smarter than their husbands. That was the local attitude. But my father expected me to learn as much as I could, to become as independent as possible, and to maintain my independence instead of being under someone's rule.

Marisol continued to work hard to achieve her education, even though her home life became consumed with physical and mental abuse. Yet her mother always reminded her of the benefits of schooling: "My mother just kept saying, 'The only way you'll have a better life is to get an education.'" However, it was the words of her 4th-grade teacher, Mr. Flores, that kept her working toward the goal of attending college: "I asked him, 'How do you become a teacher?' He said you have to graduate from high school. You have to go to college. [I wondered] how do you pay for college? He said, 'You have to graduate and get scholarships. You have to work for it.'" Mr. Flores maintained his support of Marisol as the year progressed. The culture of care found within his classroom silently spoke to her, even amid personal turmoil and abuse: "And so I started learning even as a fourth grader and before long I began researching colleges. I had other folks that I worked for in high school that also guided me in my research for college, but he [Mr. Flores] got me on the road of thinking about college and setting my goal to do my best in school."

Marisol's experiences as a young child and continuing into college successfully prepared her for the opportunities found within the classroom. During Marisol's teaching career, there have always been students in need of bilingual classes but very few teachers capable of teaching in a bilingual setting. Marisol grasps this opportunity to teach in such a classroom and to give back to her culture through words, instruction, and hope for children while opening doors of understanding to families. In her classroom, she applauds her students in their search for answers, yet more importantly, she challenges them to search for their own questions. When asked what words of hope she most often shares with Hispanic students, Marisol proudly declares: "Don't forget your past; look forward to the future; and never give up."

> **TIME TO REFLECT**
>
> What role does your past play in forging your future? Did you have strong role models that influenced you and led you to your current position? If so, describe their impact upon your life.

CHOOSING TO CARE

Student achievement based upon national and state guidelines continues to be documented in many of today's schools, however true learning that stems from a personal desire to know and understand and extends beyond short-term memory does not necessarily happen without the guidance and support of caring educators. Christle, Jolivette, and Nelson (2005) identify four school-based practices that ensure academic success among students of all ages: supportive leadership, consistent school-wide behavior management, dedicated and caring faculty and staff members, and effective teaching. The investigators contend that when these qualities are present in a school, delinquent behavior that often leads to poor academic performance can be lessened.

Lawrence, Jones, and Smith (1999) interviewed elementary-aged children about what they believed to be important school factors influencing their academic success. The youngsters reported the most important was having someone who truly listens; the second factor reported, following closely behind the first, was to be given acceptance and unconditional love by a caring adult.

Many children are not fortunate enough to have parents who can or will provide for even their basic needs. Daily we hear news reports about an ever-increasing number of minors experiencing challenging situations at home. Unless we educators step away from the safety of the podium and into our students' worlds, which are often filled with pain, neglect, and abuse, we stand the chance of losing a generation of learners even as our nation continues its march toward the unrealistic quest of leaving no child behind.

The willingness to step into our children's world requires as its first step the desire to care. Caring educators have the unique opportunity to reach across societal divisions and extend helping hands to those who are in need, to offer hope to the hopeless. Yet we can only give away to others that which we possess. A greater sense of care can evolve through purposeful dialogue, deep reflection, and mindful inquiry among educators, parents, policymakers, and community members. It may seem to some a difficult and challenging task, but we as a nation really have no other choice.

A 3rd-grade teacher illustrates the importance of caring during an after-school reception for a retiring colleague: "I feel that the kids want to do well in the classroom because of the relationship that I build with them. I think the relationship factor has remained stable throughout all of the other changes." Another teacher joins in the conversation: "We have such a short amount of time to get all of the material in, but the rapport with the kids and the reality that we truly care about them will last much longer and will, hopefully, make much more of an impact in their life."

Pellicer (2003) is "convinced that if everyone in the school, working together as a cohesive unit, cares enough about the children, then together they will find out what needs to be done to make the children successful and they will do everything in their power to see that it gets done" (p. 32). He continues by asking: "How can we ever expect parents to trust and support schools with their most precious possessions, their children, unless we who work in those schools can demonstrate beyond all doubt that we genuinely and deeply care about what happens to those children?" (p. 32).

> **TIME TO REFLECT**
>
> As a body of educators, are you collectively willing to engage in purposeful dialogue, deep reflection, and mindful inquiry? If so, closely examine the current atmosphere of learning on your campus. Do you find evidence of caring and hopeful learning within the classrooms? List the evidence that you have witnessed firsthand. Identify and list areas that require focused improvement.

CONCLUSION

In Coelho's (1993) book *The Alchemist*, the following conversation occurs as the boy and the alchemist travel across the desert:

> "Why do we have to listen to our hearts?" the boy asked, when they had made camp that day. "Because, wherever your heart is, that is where you'll find your treasure."
> "But my heart is agitated," the boy said. "It has its dreams, it gets emotional, and it becomes passionate.... It asks things of me, and it keeps me from sleeping many nights." "Well, that's good. Your heart is alive. Keep listening to what it has to say." (p. 128)

Many educators can remember moments when hearts were passionate and emotional and home lights continued to burn long into the night as lesson plans were agonized over while preparing for the next day. However, too many hearts have become disconnected from the teaching process. The production and analysis of data has too often sterilized the classroom setting and removed the human quality of caring from the equation. Educators are now driven to perform and reach levels defined by national and state departments in order to garner such titles as *exemplary* and *proficient* instead of moving toward personal achievement goals. We have simply gone through the motions without forging a connection with our heart's calling.

Just last week Beth moved into a new office. As she placed her diplomas on one of the walls, she reflected on the impact each one has made on her life. Beth began with the doctoral diploma and then mentally moved further back in time to the awarding of the master's degree, followed by the bachelor's degrees. Yet the one that held her gaze the longest was the kindergarten diploma and the class picture that accompanied it. Beth's eyes were fixed on the young children found in the black-and-white image. Mrs. Calvin was stationed in the back of the classroom, smiling proudly as she stood among her cherished students.

Palmer (1990) in *The Active Life* describes caring as an individual action freely chosen. He continues: "In caring we aim not at giving birth to something new; we aim at nurturing, protecting, guiding, healing, or empowering something that already has life. The energy behind caring is compassion for others which, in turn, is energized by the knowledge that we are all in this together, that the fate of other beings has implications for our own fate" (p. 10). Mrs. Calvin would have understood what Palmer is saying if she had lived long enough to have read his work. She knew that within her little red schoolhouse there were 25 living, breathing individuals who carried within them all of the potential that could possibly be. She understood her role as educator: to nurture and guide, to heal and protect. And in so doing, she was extending her life beyond mortality into another world that she would not experience.

Graduation day at the little red schoolhouse was an exciting time for all of the children and parents. The expectation of what was to come in 1st grade held its sway on each person, yet all stood firm in the fact that many accomplishments had been achieved during that year. Beth did not know the whereabouts of many of her fellow classmates, but she did know that each life would have been vastly different had the students not been given the initial care and encouragement of Mrs. Calvin. What a foundational experience she provided each one! She had done her part in the scheme of life; it was now up to each person to follow the path of lifelong learning.

Beth received the news that her kindergarten teacher had died 10 years after this experience at the little red schoolhouse. She did not attend her funeral nor did she send a card or flowers. Beth was barely

15 years old and selfishly consumed with the life of a teenager. Yet the words of her passing did not escape her attention. She inwardly paused and remembered her life and her gift to each student. And it was Beth's hope that one day her students will pause and remember her life and gift to them, passed from one generation of caring educators to another, from this world into the world to come.

REFERENCES

Beck, L. G. (1994). *Reclaiming educational administration as a caring profession.* New York: Teachers College Press.

Bruner, J. (1996). *Culture and education.* Cambridge: Harvard University Press.

Christle, C. A., Jolivette, K., & Nelson, C. M. (2005). Breaking the school to prison pipeline: Identifying school risk and protective factors for youth delinquency. *Exceptionality, 13*(2), 69–88.

Coelho, P. (1993). *The alchemist.* San Francisco: HarperCollins.

Corbett, H. D., & Wilson, B. L. (1991). *Testing, reform, and rebellion.* Norwood, NJ: Ablex.

Firestone, W. A., Mayrowetz, D., & Fairman, J. (1998). Performance-based assessment and instructional change: The effects of testing in Maine and Maryland. *Educational Evaluation and Policy Analysis, 20*(2), 95–113.

Lawrence, W., Jones, E., & Smith, F. (1999). Students' perceived needs as identified by students. *Journal of Instructional Psychology, 26*(1), 22–29.

Noddings, N. (1992). *The challenge to care in schools: An alternative approach to education.* New York: Teachers College Press.

Oakes, J., & Lipton, M. (1999). *Teaching to change the world.* Boston: McGraw-Hill College.

Palmer, P. (1990). *The active life: A spirituality of work, creativity, and caring.* San Francisco: Harper and Row.

Pellicer, L. O. (2003). *Caring enough to lead: How reflective thought leads to moral leadership.* Thousand Oaks, CA: Corwin Press.

Smith, M. L. (1991). Put to the test: The effects of external testing on teachers. *Educational Researcher, 20*(5), 8–11.

Vygotsky, L. S. (1978). *Mind in society: The development of higher psychological processes.* Cambridge, MA: Harvard University Press.

2

A GEM IN THE MAKING

Ann Guilbert

Every person decides whether their footprints will last beyond a lifetime or sink in the sands of time.

—Leonard Sweet

For a student, there is nothing more satisfying than a teacher demonstrating confidence in his or her ability. Students often recall such experiences years after being in a learning environment that provided safety and cultivated opportunities for learning. They recall with fondness the teacher's warmth as well as his or her high expectations and steadfast commitment toward learning (Danielson 1996). Creating this type of classroom environment rests in the teacher's ability to develop the full potential of students while maintaining high levels of student achievement (Kellough & Kellough 2008).

The selected teachers in this chapter demonstrate genuine caring and respect for all children while recognizing that students must have a learning environment in which rigorous standards are a part of the teacher–student relationship. The questions that drive the teachers in this discussion then are: Will my actions within the classroom demonstrate my belief that all students can learn? How does this look in today's classroom?

MAKING A DIFFERENCE

Pat's story began on a summer day as she walked along the beach. As the waves came to shore, she noticed the impressions her feet made along the water's edge. Strategically, she created a pattern that spelled the three letters of her name only to have a large wave quickly crash the shore and wash them away. Pat continued to walk on the water's edge, thinking all along about the school year that would be starting in only 2 weeks. She thought about those waves coming ashore and completely eliminating the evidence of her standing on this ground, and Pat wondered how much of what she would teach to her students would be like those letters—just washed away.

Pat continued to reflect but this time out loud as if someone was listening, "What I do—could it be similar to what happens with the grains of sand?" She remembered her science lessons, especially those referring to the creation of minerals and gems. In her mind, she recollected that some granules bond together and make beautiful limestone that might be used to build majestic buildings. Some of them ultimately are put under enough pressure and heat that, in due time, they form a diamond—the most valuable of all gems. If she insisted that the sand stay in place and her name remained, then those pieces of sand that washed away would never have the opportunity to reach their full purpose and potential. Pat hoped to always remember this analogy while fully expecting her students to be the grain of sand that makes the gem.

After Pat left the beach and returned to town, she called a colleague and asked if they could possibly meet for lunch. Pat and Sheryl found a booth in the restaurant and sat down. Quickly the conversation turned to thoughts on school and the struggles that they both had experienced last year with their students. Pat mentioned what had occurred on the beach with her footprints and the waves and questioned her colleague about the similarity of the impact of the wave to that of the impact educators have on students. She questioned if that was the reason the phrase "we've never had this before" has been heard so frequently on their campus, even though they both knew that the teachers in preceding grades were teaching the material. Sheryl then asked, "What would it take for us to really make a difference, the kind of difference that kids need? What would it take to make sure that 'no child was left behind'?"

As they ate, they continued their dialogue about earlier years in their teaching professions. Pat recalled her nervous anticipation as she prepared to move to her first teaching assignment. She had packed up her 1978 Ford Pinto with everything that would be needed and hopped into the driver's seat. Pat's excitement was mixed with fear, as she prayed to reach at least one child during the coming year. Pat's prayer was answered but not in the way that she had anticipated. Instead of only hoping to impact one child, Pat later learned that her presence in the classroom made a difference in every child's life. Simply creating a positive atmosphere as new lessons were taught or choosing to smile and greet the students' as they changed classes proved to be another opportunity to impact a life.

Over the years, Pat had transitioned from the classroom to administrative duties. Her newer responsibilities allowed her an opportunity to visit classrooms and observe teachers as they interacted with students and created learning environments that motivate and propel students forward. Pat has noticed through her observations that the middle school teachers are doing everything within their power to keep their students from being "left behind."

As she talked to the teachers who teach in high-stakes areas and whose students do well within those areas, one recurring theme stood out. Each teacher felt that he or she should aim high while believing that the students could meet those high expectations with guidance and assistance: "They can do what teachers expect as long as those teachers are willing to scaffold the learning or provide a differentiated learning experience."

What a teacher believes about his or her students' abilities to succeed in school influences the interaction with each one and in turn impacts the level of achievement students attain. If a teacher believes the students will succeed, he or she will behave in a manner that will allow the student to succeed. If he or she does not believe the students can succeed, then that teacher will act on that belief in negative ways. The power of this dynamic in the classroom remains one of the most important predictors of success or failure simply because it is a belief that subtly emerges from the teacher (Marzano 2007).

> **TIME TO REFLECT**
>
> What do you believe about your students' abilities within the classroom? What actions do teachers have that communicate that they believe students can and will learn? Compare your mannerisms to those of your action list. Discuss the idea of a self-fulfilling prophecy. How can teachers support a student's learning in a way to intercede for the student so that failure does not become an option?

MANAGING EXPECTATION AND ROUTINE

Teaching is described by many as both an art and a science (Marzano 2007). As striking and memorable classroom experiences merge together in one's mind, an element of art emerges from this mental collage, showcasing personal learning and expectations. These images create within the teacher a place of reflection, as one contemplates on what was and what will be. A seasoned teacher thinking back on his or her earlier years can now visualize and understand the relationship of student expectations and achievement, as well as instructional skills and strategies and students' engagement.

Promising teachers begin to develop early in their careers a level of expectation for student work that leads to creative ways of teaching, allowing students to achieve at higher levels. As more is learned about the act of teaching, one understands and believes that students can accomplish whatever is required of them.

Good and Nichols (2001) examine the possibilities of achievement when students are provided multiple opportunities in conjunction with a higher level of expectation. Their study characterizes students whose test scores preempted them from participating in prealgebra classes but were allowed to enroll simply because a teacher believed in their capabilities. Grades were tracked over a period of time, and results of the more advanced course content and higher teacher expectations were associated with positive student achievement, providing all students with opportunities to continue enrolling in advanced-level mathematics courses. The study documents higher overall scores in these classes when compared to a group of students who were denied access to prealgebra.

A culture of high student expectations and achievement requires the teacher to manage certain elements before good instruction is possible. Before school even begins, teachers must devote time to developing processes and procedures that allow for a smooth flow of the classroom, while ensuring efficient use of time within the instructional setting. When students understand where they are to go and what they are to do, time can be used much more efficiently, and learning can be maximized. Danielson (1996) notes that "In a well-managed classroom, procedures and transitions are seamless, and students assume responsibility for the classroom's smooth operation" (p. 70). Teachers who have acquired the skill of classroom management can maximize the momentum of learning and better use the time on instruction.

The creation of routines allows teachers to manage time and students, to distribute and collect materials, and to perform noninstructional responsibilities. Teachers who demonstrate skills in classroom management typically have found that smaller, ongoing instructional groups maximize learning. Activities with clear beginnings and endings allow students to engage, transition, and reengage on a smoother level than those without defined boundaries. Minimal time is lost when organization is present. If rituals and routines are established within the initial days of instruction and are followed consistently throughout the year, the learning time will be enhanced, and student success will improve (Danielson 1996).

> **TIME TO REFLECT**
>
> What type of classroom management procedures do you have in place that maximizes the learning of all children? What type of procedures would you like to incorporate into your classroom? What role does observing other teachers play in developing ideas for managing your classroom? Describe one or two ideas that you have gathered from other teachers, and discuss how you implemented them in your classroom. What are ways that you have of opening dialogue among your colleagues as you work together to enhance teaching skills?

ESTABLISHING CARING RELATIONSHIPS

An integral component of teaching lies in the relationships that exist between teachers and students. Marzano (2007) argues that the relational quality teachers maintain with their students establishes the cornerstone of effective management and possibly the entirety of teaching. Such relationships are fundamentally grounded in rapport and mutual respect between and among students and teachers. This collegial environment is created through the interactions that occur on a daily basis. In a respectful environment, individuals feel valued and safe. School community members know they will be treated with dignity even as they take intellectual risks (Kellough & Kellough 2008).

Candy

Candy teaches mathematics in a middle school setting, specifically working with 7th-graders. As classes change, one can hear Candy encouraging the students to hurry and get seated so that they can begin their work. Students understand that when they enter this classroom, they will immediately get started on the warm-up activity. Candy does not have to remind the children daily because she consistently maintains that level of expectation throughout the school year: "Getting students into a pattern, and then following that pattern everyday let's them know I mean business and my business is learning."

Many of her students have been unsuccessful in earlier grades, especially in math classes. However, Candy's constant reminder that each child can succeed in math, as well as in life, sinks in. Her care and concern builds their self-esteem and confidence and pays off for many as the grading period ends. She remarks that she cannot stop when only their weaknesses have been identified; she must also identify their strengths.

Candy's demeanor is often viewed by outsiders as a sergeant barking orders in a strict, businesslike voice, yet her students understand that this gruff persona is simply her way of expressing a deeper emotion. One student remarks, "When our teacher ceases to remind us of the quality of our work, of constantly trying to improve upon what we did yesterday, then we will know she has ceased to care about us."

One of Candy's former students recently emailed her, "It may have looked like I wasn't listening, but I was. In fact, your expectation of my work paid off when I took the state test in math and scored a proficient. I don't think I could've done it without you." Candy's response was, "Wow! Things like that blow you away and just reassure me that what I am doing is working."

Kathy

Kathy, a 6th-grade language arts teacher at the same school, stands quietly at her classroom door, chatting with students as they enter: "I stand at the door everyday as part of my routine. When I extend my hand to welcome them, their response is a good indicator of how I need to respond to them as we work together in class. Students function best when little things in the classroom become a routine expectation of mine. Even though they may be little, they still set boundaries of expectations that I consistently enforce."

The classroom is an exciting place for each person, as Kathy's students concentrate on the day's lesson and look for opportunities to share their findings with anyone willing to listen. Their work remains proudly displayed in the classroom as a testimonial of their abilities and their fascination with the content.

Kathy has two degrees, one in special education and another in elementary education, and they have worked in her favor as the individualized instructional strategies used in a special education classroom have transferred effectively into her regular education classroom. The approaches are geared to meet an individual exactly where his or her are abilities are, and as demonstrated in her 6th-grade classroom, this approach is working. The challenge is maintaining that high level of expectation throughout the school year; however, Kathy believes that there really is no other choice.

Rubie-Davies (2007) believes that today's classroom environment must be one that cultivates learning and encourages high-quality work. To accomplish this, there must be high expectations for *all* students, as well as the assurance of a safe environment for taking risks. Students in these classrooms do not fear ridicule when they put forward an idea that is atypical (Rubie-Davies, Hattie, & Hamilton 2006). In fact, student–teacher interactions are often characterized by a full expenditure of best effort and deep cultivation of thinking.

TIME TO REFLECT

Think about your teachers in elementary, middle, or high school. What type of impact did they have on your ability to learn? Did these people encourage you to go beyond your capacities and excel in areas you never thought possible? Or did they instill within you guidelines and parameters of social expectations while at the same time helping you to see your place in this world? If you were to write a letter to any teacher, what would you say? Would there be a connection made with the management of the classroom and the amount of learning that you experienced?

REFUSING TO ALLOW FAILURE

In this atmosphere of high-stakes testing, students are achieving in the classrooms of those teachers who have decided that there is not an option to fail. These teachers have established a strong work ethic for themselves and set goals that make a difference in the learning environment. Before they walk into the classroom, they have set goals to impact every student's life positively. The instruction then is designed in such a way that both student and teacher reach the goals.

At the heart of instruction is a teacher who is clear and consistent with expectations and who establishes a relationship with each student. The extra measure of high expectation is followed by a support system of scaffolded instruction and differentiation. The design of the environment allows students to experience a safe, orderly, and consistent environment.

The relationships that are established encourage a strong bond and engrave a message of confidence and courage on the student. Students of these teachers recognize the impact they have had on their learning and can communicate their appreciation for the extra motivation that was instilled. When they move into another stage of life, they recognize that the level of expectation in that classroom was a key to open the door to their success.

REFERENCES

Danielson, C. (1996). *Enhancing professional practice: A framework for teaching.* Alexandria, VA: Association for Supervision and Curriculum Development.

Good, T., & Nichols, S. (2001). Expectancy effects in the classroom: A special focus on improving the reading performance of minority students in first-grade classrooms. *Educational Psychologist, 36,* 113–126.

Kellough, R., & Kellough, N. (2008). *Teaching young adolescents: A guide to methods and resources.* 5th ed. Columbus, OH: Prentice Hall.

Marzano, R. (2007). *The art and science of teaching.* Alexandria, VA: Association for Supervision and Curriculum Development.

Rubie-Davies, C. (2007). Classroom interactions: Exploring the practices of high- and low-expectation teachers. *British Journal of Educational Psychology, 77,* 289–306.

Rubie-Davies, C., Hattie, J., & Hamilton, R. (2006). Expecting the best for students: Teacher expectation and academic outcomes. *British Journal of Educational Psychology, 76,* 429–444.

❸

CARING IN AN AGE OF ACCOUNTABILITY

Nelda Wellman

> Caring is the very bedrock of all successful education and . . . contemporary schooling can be revitalized in its light.
>
> —Nel Noddings

We live in an era in which students know more about methamphetamine than the history of our country; genealogy is no longer represented by a family tree but a series of tangled vines. As the family unit slips into obsolescence, enduring relationships with responsible adults are becoming more difficult for children to maintain. Educators face situations that could easily require a counselor's degree, as they work with students through mounds of emotional baggage.

Depending upon the age of the students, many find it difficult to effectively communicate their feelings to an adult. Trained professionals have long understood the benefits of writing as a means of observing the inner workings of a child. Today, educators have found its usefulness as a method of student self-expression, and since writing is strongly encouraged in all subject areas, multiple opportunities exist for students to reflect upon and write about delicate issues.

WRITING AS A MEANS OF BRIDGING

Writing serves a multitude of purposes, therefore it can easily become a skill used throughout life. One of the major purposes of writing is to synthesize ideas, concepts, and knowledge; another purpose is a means of purification or cleansing. As individuals are encouraged to express internal feelings and emotions, writing can be extremely productive in dealing with conflict. As with any new project, a time of instruction is needed to assist students in the formation of skills related to the resolution process. This process could help in the development and promotion of lifelong conflict management skills. Through the teaching of a few simple writing elements, such as the reflecting-and-responding method, topics from every subject can be used to help students work through sensitive areas. By stimulating the thought process through carefully selected prompts, students are given opportunities to connect the internal with the external.

An example of a writing prompt for students studying the American Revolution in social studies might begin, "Reflect upon a time when you were involved in a conflict situation. How did you decide who stood for what was right versus what was wrong?" After providing the students a few moments in reflection, they would then be allowed to respond through writing. The teacher would then move the students into a time of deeper reflection: "What was the outcome of your choice in that particular conflict? What could you have done differently, providing you with a different outcome?" As with all writing sessions, the student would individually meet with the teacher for a discussion concerning the elements of the paper, as well as for editing. With insight, the caring teacher could also gently and patiently work to redirect the student in conflict management.

ONE TEACHER'S STORY

Suggesting hidden tears, Karen's voice begins to break as she shares the painful story of the sorrow she feels for several of her students. Karen explains,

You can't imagine what some of my students have experienced even at their young age. In 3 years I have witnessed one student's father kill the mother. Tragic incidents have happened to more students than I would like to admit. Things happen. Students return to class and are unable to concentrate. I wish I could do something to reach out to them. How am I expected to prepare them for a test that will determine promotion or failure when I can't even get them to concentrate on the day's activities?

Karen continues to share about her students and their family involvement in drug raids or family members incarcerated for a variety of crimes. Karen finds it almost impossible to connect with her students in a meaningful way: "I care deeply about each one of them, but I cannot give back to them the things that they have lost. I feel helpless and hopeless."

PSYCHOLOGICAL AND SOCIAL EFFECTS OF POVERTY

Karen's deeply emotional story is a reminder that not all students have equal opportunities for success in the educational setting. Outside factors enter into the equation of equity and justice, yet the same factors fail to enter into the equation of high-stakes testing. Kincheloe and Steinberg (1999) reiterate this concept when they state that we are never independent of social and historical forces surrounding us, therefore we are unable to be separated from the contextual, from those forces that created them. The psychological and emotional scars upon the mind and heart of students who have witnessed such atrocities might perhaps never find complete healing.

Students such as these are generally situated in homes of lower socioeconomic status and high poverty levels. Thus, many enter kindergarten with a distinct disadvantage. A large percent of students maintain a limited perspective on life, having never traveled beyond the local neighborhood. Many students come from single-parent homes and are often born into a welfare-dependent world.

Miranda (1991) links lower socioeconomic status to educational performance, stating that this group of students is often developmentally delayed when compared to students of the same age from distinctly different backgrounds. She also gives credence to an earlier study of increased dropout rates among students from a lower socioeconomic group, thus continuing the cycle of poverty.

Payne (1995) identifies a wide range of contributing factors within the framework of poverty, noting that poverty is relative and can occur in all races. She acknowledges two primary types of poverty: generational and situational. Generational poverty is defined by Payne as "having been in poverty for at least two generations" (p. 101). Situational poverty is defined as having a "lack of resources attributable to a particular event" (p. 102), such as death, illness, or divorce. Sadly enough, Payne notes that from the perspective of poverty, "it is expected that [children] will go to prison just as their fathers before them, and in some cases their mothers" (p. 121).

As if these factors are not enough, additional circumstances are likely to occur in their lives. Not only are children in poverty more likely to be raised in single-parent homes, but they are more likely to be victims of child abuse or neglect when compared to children from higher socioeconomic groups. However, as Payne (1995) points out, "Being in poverty is rarely about a lack of intelligence or ability"; rather it seems to be associated with the fact that they simply don't understand there is a choice in the matter and a belief that one can move from one class into another (p. 125).

BUILDING BRIDGES TO SUCCESS

Physical bridges come in all shapes, materials, and sizes and are used for a variety of purposes; however, they require careful planning and preparation on the developer's part. First, a secure and stable foundation must be prepared because without a proper foundation, the bridge would collapse under its own weight. Materials must be carefully selected, otherwise the bridge could not sustain the forces that will definitely come against it. Time and energy must be expended in the actual building process, and one day, the bridge will be complete and ready to use.

The same steps required to build physical bridges are also necessary in the construction of relational bridges. These bridges can also be as varied as those found dotting our landscape. Some may be suspension bridges, while others may be footbridges. A sure foundation mortared together with genuineness and truthfulness secures the structure that is to come. Time and energy are also required as individuals come to know and trust each other. Ultimately, the relational bridge is completed, and we find a solid connection in place.

This analogy applies to caring teachers who are seeking to connect with their students. Young people clearly understand when an adult is attempting to demonstrate genuine concern and understanding, as opposed to when an adult's actions are insincere. Positive relational communication must include the acknowledgment of the cultural setting of students, as well as their values, shared beliefs, interests, and accepted attitudes and behaviors that originate from that setting. As the bridge moves ever closer toward completion, the teacher and student witness transformational change within themselves and each other.

In the poem "A Noiseless Patient Spider," Whitman colorfully explains the building of a spider's web. Anchor points are needed to ensure the support of the web. Once they are securely in place, additional strands then connect one point to another. Whitman wrote, "It launch'd forth filament, filament, filament, out of itself, Ever unreeling them, ever tirelessly speeding them. . . . Till the bridge you will need be form'd, till the ductile anchor hold." Whitman suggests this continual building process through the ceaseless "musing, venturing, throwing, seeking the spheres to connect them." So it is in relational bridges.

Caring teachers bridge the gap through communication while encouraging a transparency in the daily classroom interaction and exchange. The positive reaction of such a powerful force brings about a feeling of security. As the student relaxes amid the safety of the bond, previous negative behaviors disappear. This conversion provides the impetus necessary for an improved future for all involved.

REACHING OUT THROUGH CARING RELATIONSHIPS

There is no doubt that Karen is, in fact, a caring and nurturing teacher, even though she is overwhelmed by a sense of helplessness as she tries to span the gulf between an abusive home and the loving classroom. All too often teachers are required to become the anchor for their students as they look for something or someone to save them. The relational bridging concept provides constancy and connection for those confused about life.

Wheatley (2002) clarifies, "We are interconnected to all life" (p. 6). This interconnectedness from one generation to another can provide the mirror that will illuminate care in an uncaring world. Wheatley further expounds, "We act on this truth when we're willing to notice how a decision might affect others, when we try to think systemically, when we're willing to look down the road and notice how, at this moment, we might be affecting future generations" (p. 6). The opportunity of teachers to influence children today and tomorrow creates an amazing world of possibility. Noddings (1992) points out that a "school cannot achieve its academic goals without providing caring and continuity for students" (p. 14). If this is true, then our classrooms must become more, more than a place to prepare students for a test, more than desks and chalkboards.

> **TIME TO REFLECT**
>
> What are your thoughts on this "interconnectedness" to life? Reflect upon your own personal life and the connections that have been made from childhood until now. Do we really understand the impact one small decision may have on our connections (e.g., family members, students)? Create a visual image of your own personal connections, and see where it takes you.

SUSTAINING THE RELATIONSHIP THROUGH CARING

Karen thought about how she might better prepare her students, especially in regard to the high-stakes testing movement. With a realization of the need for relational bridging, she felt pressured to build connections while at the same time building her students' level of knowledge and skills. Karen asked herself numerous times what would be the most important to learn, what would serve them the best in their future. She leaned toward the efficacy of care.

Payne (1995) takes the concept of caring relationships further: "No significant learning occurs without a significant relationship" (p. 211–212). Even as one seeks to understand poverty, relationships remain a necessary objective because they are the "most significant motivator for the students" (p. 212). Karen was intrigued about Payne's explanation of how relationships could be developed and reasoned "through support systems, through caring about students, by promoting student achievement, by being role models, by insisting upon successful behaviors for school" (p. 217). This brings credence to Karen's thoughts and feelings as they relate to her struggling students. However, she also understood that within the educational system, there remains a stronger focus on assessments and accountability rather than on the development of the whole child.

Doyle and Doyle (2003) speak of those schools that have somehow embraced the notion of care, moving beyond the content and entering the psychological and social realm of well-being. Karen sensed a ray of hope as she read further. Her sense of knowing what was right was proven as she found evidence that pointed to relationships being regarded as necessary to learning. Freire (2002) mentions that a caring and loving attitude is developed through relationships, and these relationships can and should begin in the classroom.

CARING IN AN AGE OF ACCOUNTABILITY

It is often difficult for teachers to remain focused on their main responsibility, which is to teach children how to think and learn for themselves instead of preparing them for an accountability test. Outside pressures demanding quantifiable successes, as well as the realization that they—teachers—are also being measured for success creates an "end product" mentality. This mentality creates tunnel vision, while greatly limiting the development of the "whole child." The question then becomes, How can teachers merge the attitude of care with the pressure of performing in such a way that it proves beneficial to students and teachers alike?

There are three defined ways to accomplish this task: (1) Build positive relationships among faculty and staff members, (2) develop and maintain positive and supportive connections with school administrators, and (3) seek to create an attitude of care within the classroom and school. While the three steps toward improving relationships within a school maintain similar characteristics, there remain distinct differences, one of which involves the intentional development of positive relationships among faculty and staff, including school administrators.

Building positive relationships with fellow teachers, staff, and administrators may seem insignificant, however these relationships provide the support base and encouragement from which all other work flows. This foundation produces a morale that can help sustain teachers, especially during stressful times. An added effect of such positive relationships proves to be instrumental in modeling this attitude of care to the students. They, in turn, will often pick up on such demonstrations and will begin to portray care to their peers. An attitude of civility for mankind will emerge, spilling over into the community. It proves to be a win-win situation for all involved.

ANCHORING RELATIONSHIPS THROUGH THE WRITING PROCESS

Teachers often ask the same question that Karen posed: "How can I ever prepare my students for all that they must experience when I am not even sure what that may be?" Just as Noddings (1992) argues that caring and continuity must be in place for student academic achievement to occur, so must Karen first provide the nurturing necessary in the building of relationships. Dialogue with each student is the beginning stage in the process of care as trust is established. The invitation to write serves as this entry point, allowing teacher and student an opportunity to learn more about each other.

The writing process allows the student to be expressive about feelings and emotions that might otherwise be repressed. Early in the school year, students are hesitant to let others into their thoughts and minds for fear of exposing too much. But as the relationship develops, writing becomes a tool in which the child can work through feelings and fears. Often teachers may find their children in need of trained professionals who are more qualified in dealing with intense levels of grief, loss, and anger. This does not imply that the teacher has failed; rather, he or she has identified the proper resources necessary in helping the student. That in itself is a reflection of care on the part of the teacher.

Most school districts are now promoting a writing component in all subject areas as a means to synthesize learning and to integrate other subjects. What better way to teach the constructs of writing while at the same time reaching one who might be socially and psychologically struggling.

> **TIME TO REFLECT**
>
> Reflect on the writing program within your school. Does it provide an opportunity for the student to openly share thoughts, feelings, and hopes for the future? Or is it merely one that reiterates the three-step method used in many of today's standardized tests? Have you ever considered this as an opportunity to learn more about your students and them you? Begin a dialogue on your campus about your school's attitude of care, and determine possible steps needed to demonstrate this sentiment to all children.

REFERENCES

Doyle, L. H., & Doyle, P. M. (2003). Building schools as caring communities: Why, what, and how? *The Clearing House*, pp. 259–260.

Freire, P. (2002). *Pedagogy of the oppressed.* New York: Continuum International.

Kincheloe, J. L., & Steinberg, S. R. (1999). A tentative description of post-formal thinking: The critical confrontation with cognitive theory. In S. R. Steinberg, J. L. Kincheloe, & P. H. Hinchey (Eds.), *The postformal reader: Cognition and education* (pp. 55–90). New York: Falmer Press.

Miranda, L. C. (1991). *Latino child poverty in the United States.* Washington, DC: Children's Defense Fund.

Noddings, N. (1992). *The challenge to care in schools: An alternative approach to education.* New York: Teachers College Press.

Payne, R. K. (1995). *A framework for understanding and working with students and adults from poverty.* Baytown, TX: RFT.

Wheatley, M. J. (2002). *Turning to one another: Simple conversations to restore hope to the future.* San Francisco: Berrett-Koehler.

4

THE TRANSFORMATIVE POWER OF RELATIONSHIPS

Wendell Wellman

We can never assume anyone sees the world as we do.

—Margaret Wheatley

The counselor stood on the sidewalk as he watched the Child Protective Services car drive away with two of his students in the back seat. Matthew, 12 years old, and Susan, 9 and in the 3rd grade, were both staring at Mr. Thomas through the car's side window as tears continued to streak their reddened faces. A voice inside of Mr. Thomas's head kept repeating, "Well, just punish them! Don't put up with it!" Through the harsh and condemning words came sounds of tenderness: "Those who need love the most deserve it the least" and "Your most difficult student is the one who needs you the most!" The evil and the good were a constant reminder of the events leading up to this scene.

Matthew and Susan had enrolled 6 months earlier in a rural K–12 school consisting of approximately 400 students. Within their first week at Mendenhall County School, both students had received their first referral to Mr. Thomas's office with similar teacher notes that read, "There is no way that this student will be ready for the state test. S/he is so far behind and is making no attempt to catch up. Her/his attitude is awful!" He opened the files that had accompanied both students and found a father in the military and a mother who had left years earlier. Before the end of the first grading period, the stack of referrals had mounted, and Mr. Thomas knew that something must be done.

Both Matthew and Susan were below grade level and defiant toward authority figures. The Mendenhall County School System had been able to maintain a lower student-to-teacher ratio than the surrounding districts, which had seemingly helped many below-average students, however Matthew and Susan were failing to respond to any attempts of improving their academic status. There also continued to be a strong wall of defensiveness, translating into opposition directed toward anyone trying to help.

During one of the many visits to the counselor, Matthew was asked why he was so defensive. Mr. Thomas continued to push the boy for an answer until eventually Matthew shouted, "My dad said you would be mean to us!" He then began screaming and crying, refusing to listen to anything else Mr. Thomas said. At his wit's end and amid what appeared to be a hopeless situation, the counselor mumbled, "Alright, fine, you leave me no choice. I am just going to have to punish you because there is nothing left to do! I have reached my limit!"

Through either a strange coincidence or divine providence, the school counselor's father owned several rental properties within the Mendenhall County School System. Upon their arrival in the town, Matthew and Susan's dad opted to rent a house from the senior Mr. Thomas. This particular rental house was situated next door to the counselor's dad.

One afternoon while visiting his dad, the conversation shifted toward Matthew and Susan. The senior Mr. Thomas casually mentioned, "Those folks sure are strange. Covering the windows in one of the bedrooms are black sheets, and inside there are loads of photographic equipment. I've noticed a lot of people during all hours of the night, too." Immediately upon hearing his dad describe the scene, the counselor became troubled and began to speculate what might be occurring there.

While driving back to his own home, Mr. Thomas determined that he must call Child Protective Services and request an inspection of the home. He picked up the receiver and dialed the number. The raid on the house came sometime during the morning hours while the children were attending school. Matthew and Susan's dad and six other men were arrested. Videos had been confiscated as proof of the child pornography ring and would be used against the adults in the upcoming trial. It was determined that Matthew and Susan would be removed from the home.

As the car pulled away from the school, Matthew and Susan watched Mr. Thomas standing there. In their mind, Mr. Thomas and all the adults in the Mendenhall County School System were evil and had no right in removing them from their home. Mr. Thomas, even though he realized that what was taking place was right, felt that a wrongdoing had been done. He wished that the faculty and staff could have somehow connected with them, establishing a relationship of trust. But where there had been no trust in the home, there could be no trust in the school.

Courage to do that which is right sometimes causes despair, but even in its midst can one also find hope. Mr. Thomas sought this hope as he reflected upon relationships with other students. Many had known success through a continued dialogue and dedicated commitment to the educational process, as parents, teachers, and students work together to heal and to strengthen the relational ties. Mr. Thomas had to trust that Matthew and Susan would come to understand and eventually find hope even in their own situation.

> **TIME TO REFLECT**
>
> Have you ever experienced a time of challenge within the classroom, a time when the correct decision was not an easy one to make? As the decision was made to act, where did you find the inner strength needed to make the call? Relationships are important within today's classrooms. What characteristics do you believe make up any significant relationship? How do you go about establishing and maintaining significant relationships with your students?

EMPOWERING RELATIONSHIPS FOR PERFORMANCE

Relationships that empower are grounded in trust and offer recognition in diversity, as the uniqueness of a person is accepted and even honored. If one truly seeks to understand another, the results are usually astonishing. Wheatley (2002) explains that we label others and ourselves in an attempt to understand, with the end result being that we actually understand each other less. Wheatley continues, "We stick labels on ourselves [while] we ask others what theirs are. We assume we know each other the moment we hear the label [but] we know less about each other [though] we assume [to] know more" (p. 114).

One's personal identity is a composite of all experiences. Kincheloe and Steinberg (1999) believe that cognitive development is not static but interactive with the environment, "always in the process of being reshaped and reformed" (p. 60). Therefore, if knowledge is based on experiences, then our relationships—which provide deeper experiences—must affect our knowledge and thinking. If a school's sole purpose is to simply impart knowledge, then relationships between the teacher and the student are unnecessary. However, if knowledge is relational and relationships extend all experiences, then teacher–student relationships are critical. For knowledge to flow and truly affect the learner, as well as the instructor, relationships such as those being discussed must exist prior to the teaching. Otherwise, the content will fail to extend beyond the blackboard or the textbook and connect with the person.

> **TIME TO REFLECT**
>
> Examine the types of relationships found within your school. Do you find them to be positive, enhancing the learning experiences of all students? Or do you find them to be either sterile or negative, preventing the learning experiences from occurring?

Palmer (1993) believes that the seed of knowledge takes root within the passion of a human soul. If this is true, then the educator must continue to seek new perspectives, new solutions, and new insights as he or she comes to know his or her students on a deeper level. This understanding comes about through the establishment of relationships.

Rodgers (2002) describes reflective thinking as the process of making sense or meaning out of an experience. As an educator internally reflects, the process allows for an opportunity to make meaning out of the experience, thus moving the person through a series of spirals linking one experience to another. The result is typically a deeper understanding of connected relationships found within the experience.

Critical thinking found within a reflective moment is more than just a set of defined skills; it embodies one's character and spirit (Bolman & Deal 2001). This type of introspective thought is based on the necessity of educational accountability, but instead of the accountability coming about through government-regulated testing, it comes about through a moral and ethical calling. An educator's integrity is also grounded in consideration of others. Teachers stand before their students seeking to understand as they connect meaning to content. Schools must be environments that encourage this understanding of oneself, for the purpose of education is to make lives more meaningful. Without that foundational understanding, life will be less than it could be. Human beings were made to relate to others, as well as to passionately pursue purpose. Therefore, schools must find a way to affirm those found within its walls. If accountability must exist, then let it exist there.

> **TIME TO REFLECT**
>
> Do you believe in the notion of accountability? How could a school make itself accountable to the relationships that are found within its walls? Are there opportunities for teachers and students to passionately pursue purpose? What would this resemble if it were allowed to occur?

MEANING IN RELATIONSHIPS

Tieger and Barron-Tieger (2001) find that satisfaction lies in knowing who you are and in enjoying what you are doing. Because people have diverse needs, desires, skills, and values, it is vital for the educator to understand the whole person. It is also just as important that individuals know themselves.

Bolman and Deal (2001) point out that as human beings find meaning in their work through successful engagement in the job place, a deeper faith in self, a confidence in core values, and a hope for the future emerge. In direct contrast, if we are not able to find meaning in our life work, then we are relegated to an existence void of purpose and passion. Sokolow (2002) asks a very pointed question: Why do we work? And just as quickly he provides an answer: Because it is who we are. Therefore relationships within the work setting, whether with our students or colleagues, seemingly enhance the setting and provide for all involved a joy in the journey.

Schools in which sound relationships have developed realize that individuals are not pitted against one another within the competitive arena. However the current testing movement tends to do just that—it forces a comparison of similar students, teachers, and schools against those in the state and nation, thus creating two groups: those who can and those who can't. This mentality of us against them can destroy any hope of advancing the cause of education and virtually wipes away the love of learning from hearts and souls. Our relationships within the classrooms of today should be the result of spontaneous and creative dancing instead of war.

> **TIME TO REFLECT**
>
> What are your thoughts on the current testing environment? Have you observed both positive and negative results emerge? Do you see a mentality of success and failure perpetuating itself in and among the teachers, students, and schools where you live? Is this occurring in the primary or secondary grades or both? What affect is this having on your students and on you?

Many students have come to experience the freedom to become as they work and learn within the safety net of stable and trustworthy relationships. These relationships carry with them no conditions, only experiences. As communication allows individuals to interact with words as well as through actions, the meaning of who we are is changed. If the communication is positive, then so is the change. Similarly, if the communication is negative or demeaning, then the individual changes, too. Body language can be interpreted as one having positive or negative self-esteem. Grades may indicate an internal change as they climb or drop over time. Testing procedures can also communicate whether one child is expected to excel or fail. Often, the educator reaps what they are expecting to sow, putting into motion once again the self-fulfilling prophecy. Palmer

(1999) reiterates the fact that as educators, we have witnessed the price paid for a system of fear and possible failure. Many students have become disconnected with the learning process and have relinquished creativity and passion for compliancy.

When a classroom enters into a relationship of significance, the entire learning community finds meaning and importance. This gift provides for needs to be met, such as the need to be loved, to be listened to, and to be accepted unconditionally. Today's society has shifted from the neighborhood mentality, where families know those living next door and down the street, to an isolated and sterile environment. Relationships are managed via the Internet rather than face to face. The lack of connection with others has left many of our children engaging in destructive and violent behaviors.

Untold numbers of influences, circumstances, and people have influenced you to become who you are in this present moment. Just as the grains of sand upon the shore cannot be counted, neither can one individual count all of the influences upon his or her life. So it is in your classroom. The lives within your school are being shaped by all that occurs to them, and as an educator, you are seen as a primary shaper. The responsibility given to you is tremendous, yet the reward is beyond measure—and beyond being calculated with today's data.

TIME TO REFLECT

Think about the connections made on a daily basis in your classroom and school. Are they positive in nature or negative? If positive, evaluate the outcomes seen in your students. Do you sense that they are engaged in the learning process? Do they feel that their voice is important? Do you provide each child with an opportunity to offer something back to his or her classmates and to you?

REFERENCES

Bolman, L. G., & Deal, T. (2001). *Leading with soul: An uncommon journey of spirit.* San Francisco: Jossey-Bass.

Kincheloe, J. L., & Steinberg, S. R. (1999). A tentative description of post-formal thinking: The critical confrontation with cognitive theory. In S. R. Steinberg, J. L. Kincheloe, & P. H. Hinchey (Eds.), *The post-formal reader: Cognition and education* (pp. 55–90). New York: Falmer Press.

Palmer, P. J. (1993). *To know as we are known: Education as a spiritual journey.* New York: HarperCollins.

Palmer, P. J. (1999). Evoking the spirit in public education. *Educational Leadership, 56*(4), 6–11.

Rodgers, C. (2002). Defining reflection: Another look at John Dewey and reflective thinking. *Teachers College Record, 104*(4), 842–866.

Sokolow, S. L. (2002). Enlightened leadership. *School Administrator, 59*(8), 32–36.

Tieger, P. D., & Barron-Tieger, B. (2001). *Do what you are.* New York: Little, Brown.

Wheatley, M. J. (2002). *Turning to one another: Simple conversations to restore hope to the future.* San Francisco: Berrett-Koehler.

5

DO WHAT THEY SAY, SAY WHAT THEY MEAN: ONE THING LEADS TO ANOTHER

Sherry Durham

> We set sail on this new sea because there's knowledge to be gained.
>
> —John F. Kennedy

ACTIONS SPEAK

Campus discipline is an important part of a successful learning environment. The number of office referrals and expulsions of students are reported within the accountability measures of accepted yearly progress, a federal accountability system, and within state systems of accountability. Usually it is the duty of the assistant principal to enforce campus expectations for behavior during the school day. This seems simple enough: Make sure the students know the rules, handle each case of misbehavior as it arises, and deal with the behavior quickly and fairly. Often, the lessons learned by the adult rather than the student lead to a better campus environment and more opportunities for influential practice by the administrator involved.

Arlene is the assistant principal on a bilingual campus of 815 students. After having served as assistant principal for a middle school with a population of 1,865 students in grades 6 through 8, she decided to move to an elementary campus. The behavior problems she encountered at the middle school level were usually severe, often resulting in expelling students from the campus. She was excited about the possibilities offered to affect the lives of children on a campus of children in kindergarten through 5th grade. Little did she know that her first year would be a learning experience for her as well as for the students during the school year.

Each morning, one of Arlene's duties was announcements over the schoolwide intercom. These daily rituals of campus event reminders, menu readings, and pledges to state and country ended with a daily promise the students repeated together as a campus body to do their best, work hard, and obey school rules. What a great way to start each day with a reminder of the expectations of school personnel and parents. However, as Arlene relates, it takes more to keep the discipline in check on a campus than the district policy manual, the school mission statement, and a mantra of expectations for daily behavior.

CALL FOR ATTENTION

James was in kindergarten, but his behaviors were those of a child much younger. His younger sister was severely handicapped, and his family was very much involved in her medical and physical needs. In order for James to receive attention, he believed he needed to act out, and this he did—very well.

His kindergarten teacher was experienced and kind. She offered him every opportunity to comply with her rules, yet it seemed a daily ritual for her to come to the office carrying him like a sack of potatoes. He would refuse to walk or engage in any way with her requests for him to follow her directives to improve his behavior. On one particular day, James was screaming loudly, tears streaming down his face. He was not in any pain, nor was he being mistreated. His wailing stemmed from the fact that he was physically being forced to comply with his teacher's instructions to stop pulling down his pants and exposing his rear end. The teacher had tied a "belt" through his belt loops with a ribbon from her room to keep him from being the class exhibitionist.

Once inside the assistant principal's office, he quickly climbed under an office chair and wrapped himself around the legs in order to brace himself for the ordeal of being extricated from what he deemed to be his safe haven. No amount of begging, coaxing, or promises of calling his parents made any impact on James. Arlene was as exasperated as the teacher. A phone call to the parents was unanswered, as they were out of town with the terminally ill younger sister. It was up to the teacher and Arlene to take care of this situation. What on earth could get through to this child to not only calm him but to also get him to climb out from under the sheltering chair? Time at the middle school level certainly had not prepared Arlene for this type of intervention.

Without previous training in child psychology or strategies to deal with this type of incident, Arlene had to depend on her common sense to see her through. Using the idea of extinguishing the behavior through ignoring the situation, she asked the teacher to return to her classroom, leaving James squealing and holding onto the chair legs for dear life. After the teacher left, Arlene began to ignore James, allowing him to tire himself out with no attention, no earned interest of positive or negative concern, and no payment of frustrated and frazzled adults attempting to bring him under control.

This is often referred to as "with-it-ness." Marzano, Marzano, and Pickering (2003) describe "with-it-ness" as the "ability to identify and quickly act on potential behavior problems" (p. 75). Dealing with undesirable behaviors requires a second component in order to effectively approach the infractions. This, Marzano and colleagues share, is the ability to incorporate emotional objectivity. The two of the one-two action to change behaviors is the "ability to interact with students in a businesslike, matter of fact manner even though you may be experiencing strong emotions" (p. 75). Arlene wanted to comfort James and let him know that she was a caring element in his school life, but until he could get his behavior under control, she had to follow the guidelines she set for her expectation of compliance with school rules.

Using the same techniques she would employ for an older child, Arlene allowed James to basically wear himself out from screaming and thrashing about and then used opportunities for reflection. She calmly asked James what he had done wrong instead of having him write this down on a form, why he had engaged in the misbehavior, and what he planned to do differently next time. She used this information for a conversation about expectations for student behavior at school.

It would be nice for the story to end with James changing his behavior and seeing the error of his way once the audience was removed and he was left alone to think about his behaviors while the assistant principal went about her work in the office that morning, but alas, that would be too simple. James continued to exhibit his behaviors. However, after each offense, he was sentenced to the office area, where he would be given time to throw a tantrum and tire himself out.

The classroom teacher never deviated from the zero tolerance for his misbehaviors, but after the storm of acting out was over, she assured the student that she cared about him and wanted him to rejoin her class. The consistent enforcement of classroom rules together with time for conversation and reinforcement for desired behaviors eventually aided in decreasing the fits of resistance to classroom rules and expectations. Slowly but surely, the behaviors decreased in intensity, and a relationship of trust developed between James, his teacher, and Arlene. Sharing with the parents and encouraging them to make time for James amid their daily routine of caring for their ill child also allowed the chance for school personnel to get to know the family and suggest a support system available to them through medical services as part of a medical community in town.

In time, James was able to verbalize his feelings of anxiety and curb his attention-getting behaviors. The attention for his positive behavior began to outweigh the negative attention. James began to understand that he was wanted in the classroom and at school by his teacher, principals, and classmates and that he was valuable to the classroom.

ACTIONS OF THE HEART

Arlene also shares the lesson learned from experiencing the Wallace kids. Every teacher shuddered when their names turned up on their classroom rolls. Prior to the dreaded student setting foot inside the classroom, plans and strategies were in place for how to deal with the behaviors these children used to keep themselves and anyone in the room from having a successful learning experience.

It was common practice for their mother to come into the school's front office area to request someone to literally pull the oldest child out of the minivan. This was no small feat, as usually Larry was holding onto the frame of the car seat and kicking his legs at anyone who might dare to close in on him. More often than one wants to admit, the minivan sped away with the child still inside and his mother muttering about those folks at the school failing to get him out of the car and into the classroom.

From the administrator's point of view, it was not worth causing bodily damage to the child or self. Though his mother was asking for physical assistance, if the child were in any way harmed, the circumstances might quickly change, with the school personnel seen as being too forceful. The attitude of parents is often that it is the school's responsibility to ensure the child's attendance, when it is the parent who is held accountable.

Clearly, the call for help from the parent was heard, but instead of wanting to partner with the school to help take care of the problem, this parent continually wanted to dump all of the blame on the school for not being able to drag the child from the vehicle. Whitaker (2004) speaks about the need to extend respect to the parent but not at our expense as educators. When blasted with a barrage of rudeness or blame, he tells us to "remain professional" and "take responsibility for changing situations . . . that have led to problems. . . . Focus on the future more than on the past" (p. 29).

Working with the parent to encourage her to become consistent in taking control of the morning drop-off situations, Arlene made progress by looking for a future solution to the problem instead of revisiting the daily failures to get Larry out of the car. This resulted in new opportunities to support and make suggestions to the parent, which eventually led to Larry realizing his mom meant business when she asked him to get out of the car. After many trips from school back home, where he was quarantined from activities and made to stay inside the house, he began to open the door of the car and exit on his own accord. School didn't seem like such a bad place if staying home meant that he lost his choice to play or wander outdoors.

> **TIME TO REFLECT**
>
> Have you turned situations into opportunities to work with parents? Do you look toward the future or focus on past student behaviors? How could taking the positive approach make a difference for children?

Getting Larry to exit the car in the morning did not mean that the behavior problems with this student ended in the driveway of the school. He was often in trouble with his teacher for talking out of turn, leaning back in his chair, or failing to return a homework paper. There were no major disturbances within the classroom setting, yet enough of a noncompliance to cause a teacher who clearly displayed her dislike of this child to send him to the office for disciplinary action.

> **TIME TO REFLECT**
>
> Are there students in your classroom that you tolerate infractions of the rules from more than others? How do you react to these students? Have you recognized this behavior in yourself previously?

For some reason, Arlene liked this kid. He was not rude. He displayed honesty regardless of the consequences and made no apologies for his dislike of schooling. It was his dream to be able to stay at home with his grandfather, walk in the woods, and hunt and fish. As Arlene spent time with this child, she realized he had some anxiety issues and that his home life put him under a great deal of responsibility as the oldest child in a single-parent household.

LEARNING EXPERIENCES

Larry had a great deal of common sense and was very bright. This alone was not enough to satisfy the classroom teacher. She wanted complete and total compliance with her directives and daily assignments. This was not going to happen, and Arlene could see the writing on the wall. It was going to be a long year.

> **TIME TO REFLECT**
>
> Do you look beyond the behaviors in your classroom to see the child who is calling out for attention, whether it is in a positive or negative manner? Where would you begin to place the burden of ownership for misbehavior in your classroom? Does any of it belong to the teacher?

Since Larry was spending much of his school time in the office with Arlene, the campus counselor offered to allow Larry to share time in her office. The counselor wanted to offer this child the opportunity to openly discuss his feelings about school and share in designing a plan to satisfy all parties involved. In other words, Larry would discuss how the adults might invite him to want to learn and follow the rules of his teacher.

Throughout these visits, the counselor found out that Larry's father had recently returned home from being incarcerated. This helped both the counselor and Arlene to understand the desire of Larry to be at home instead of school. Due to the relationship these two administrators developed with this child, he felt comfortable to express his feelings and concerns about home and school, allowing them to make appropriate plans to intervene and offering him opportunities for support and sharing that would have otherwise been seen as only behavior outbursts and noncompliance.

> **TIME TO REFLECT**
>
> Do students call out through their misbehaviors for attention from the teachers or other adults on the campus? How is that attention interpreted?

The counselor began to work with Larry in tutoring sessions when he was with her in her office. A relationship of trust and respect developed between the two, and Larry began to actually seem to enjoy being at school. As his confidence in the academic areas increased, his interest and interaction within his regular classroom developed into a time when he was engaged in the learning processes. Slowly, his visits to the office and the counselor began to decrease.

It has been several years since Larry's educational "turnaround," but from time to time, the counselor drops by to visit with him in his middle school classroom. When she does, she sees a young man engaged in learning, doing his best to follow the school rules, and still looking forward to walking the woods with his grandfather after the school day is complete.

This change in behaviors did not occur on its own. It was the development of a trusting relationship with both of the students discussed that made the difference. In the case of James, an experienced teacher who was not afraid to delve deeper into his behavior problems taught the new administrator to take time to look deeper into the student entering her office. For Larry, a counselor and administrator were willing to take time to look for avenues to allow a student to understand the importance of education and his own value in the educational process to his class and campus.

REFERENCES

Marzano, R. J., Marzano, J. S., & Pickering, D. J. (2003). *Classroom management that works: Research-based strategies for every teacher.* Alexandria, VA: Association for Supervision and Curriculum Development.

Whitaker, T. (2004). *What great teachers do differently: 14 things that matter most.* Larchmont, NY: Eye on Education.

6

THE IMPACT OF A SINGLE LIFE

Terri Hebert

Each time a man . . . acts to improve the lot of others . . . he sends forth a tiny ripple of hope, and crossing each other from a million different centers of energy and daring, those ripples build a current that can sweep down the mightiest walls.

—Robert F. Kennedy

THE FIRST DAY ON THE JOB

Mark remembers the first time he made the 30-minute drive from his home to Washington Elementary: a typical interstate and its hum-drum scenery; a rather large, two-story mall; a regional airport; and a midsize university that had recently become part of a larger statewide system. Yet, as he made the final turn that would lead him directly to the school, his landscape suddenly changed from middle class to lower class. The homes were bleak and run down, with trash blotting the roadside. No one stirred that morning, even though the weather was pleasant. He wondered how quickly a neighborhood could change, and then he wondered about the inhabitants of the school. Would they be representative of the neighborhood, or were they bussed in from all parts of the district? It wasn't long before Mark had answers, as well as additional questions.

The principal, Mr. Skelton, welcomed him to the campus and to the family of Washington Elementary. Mark was given a quick tour of the building and the playground area; then Mr. Skelton dropped him off at the entrance to his classroom and wished him a good school year. The room was bare, with little resource material found inside. The wall color was painted neutral; the desks and chairs blended into the setting, almost making them invisible to the human eye. The students would be arriving soon, and Mark wondered what he would do with them. The school year began about 4 weeks earlier, and this class had experienced numerous substitutes until the hiring of Mark. He was fresh out of college with little experience, yet his enthusiasm did not waver. He was ready to teach reading and language arts to the small class of 4th-graders.

His mind reflected back on his interview with Mr. Skelton. During that time, he had been told that this school was designated by the district as a "target" school, which meant that there were no busses that ran to and from the building. The only students allowed into the school lived across the street in a housing development. Another mark of this unique setting was that every student was of African American descent, as were a large majority of faculty and staff. Mark and four other teachers were the only Caucasians on campus. Yet, the school maintained all of the district criteria as any other school: accountability, budgetary issues, curricular choices, and so on.

Due to the safety concerns of the neighborhood, all faculty and staff were asked to leave the campus by 4:30 P.M. each day. There were no after-school faculty meetings, no after-school parent–teacher conferences, no after-school athletic events or parties. How did the faculty get to know their students, the parents, or other teachers if they were not allowed to mingle in diverse settings?

Suddenly, the bell marking the next period sounded loud and clear and abruptly brought Mark back to reality. Shuffling of feet was heard advancing down the hallway—and then the door burst open with 15 students noisily entering the classroom. Their first impression of Mark was mainly curiosity, as they wondered if he was another sub. When the students found out that he would be their teacher for the remainder of the school year, they settled down a bit more. It seemed that a few of the students enjoyed having substitutes because they did not have to do "real work" as they described it. Others were bored and wanted the opportunity to learn like in the rest of the classes.

Mark began with introductions. He told of his background: where he came from, his educational history, and his likes and dislikes. Then he opened the floor up to the students. They all suddenly began talking at once, and Mark indicated that he would call on those with their hands raised. The students raised their hands but kept on talking, which frustrated Mark. He was not accustomed to children not doing what he had asked them to do. They were loud and often demanded to be heard over all the rest. Mark looked for a class roll but did not see one. He had no idea who these children were or, for that matter, whether they were to be in his room or in someone else's. By the end of the day, Mark was contemplating whether he had chosen the right profession.

He walked to the parking lot with an armful of textbooks, one slightly used lesson planner, a class roll, and a whistle that was given to him by the office secretary. As he threw the materials into the passenger's seat and then crawled into the driver's, he was aghast at the management of the school and the lack of resources available to faculty, staff, and students. But within his soul, he knew that somehow he would find a way to impact his children; somehow he would make a difference in their lives—even if he had to spend his own money to accomplish this promise.

> **TIME TO REFLECT**
>
> Do you remember yourself as a new teacher, not knowing what to do or when to do it? Do you remember thinking that there weren't enough materials to get the job done? Did you provide for the materials out of your personal account? Do you also remember thinking that you would make a difference in the students' lives, that you would impact their learning? Do you still have that fire inside you today? If so, how have you kept it alive? If not, where has it gone?

DIMINISHING THE "AT-RISK" LABEL

Studies have been conducted on the effects of racial segregation and schooling, as well as the effects of poverty and schooling; however, this setting in which Mark found himself had both present: high numbers of racially segregated and low socioeconomic students combined in one location—Washington Elementary. The Coleman Report (Coleman 1966) documents the relationship between the socioeconomic composition of schools and the academic achievement of their students.

Jencks (1972) continues the investigation, thus concluding that both black and white students performed better on achievement tests if they attended schools in which greater percentages of their peers were from higher socioeconomic families. A number of other, more recent studies continue to demonstrate the influence of school economic outcomes on student achievement (Caldas & Bankston 1997; Crane 1991; Entwisle, Alexander, & Olson 1997; Mayer 1991; Rumberger & Willms 1992).

The number of concerns mounted as Mark continued to learn more about his students and his school. A large percentage had been labeled in the area of reading to be at risk, based upon the previous year's achievement test scores. The National Center for Educational

Statistics (1999) reports that 40% of our nation's 4th-graders read below a basic level, yet at Mark's school, 60% of the 4th-graders had been labeled below basic and in need of specialized assistance. What were these students to do and how could they be successful in a school setting if they were unable to read simple text? These children were destined for failure in today's global society unless something extraordinary was done. They and their families were marginalized in every conceivable way: educationally, socially, and economically. Yet, the school system continued to place them in an isolated school and create tests that encompassed grade-level material far above their current level and failed to provide adequate materials to support the required curriculum.

During the summer months, Mark became a frequent guest of a local university library as he researched similar school settings. He wanted to enter his classroom in August armed with current findings and reliable strategies necessary to boost his students' abilities. While visiting the library one evening, he saw a flyer posted on a bulletin board beside the entrance. It announced an opportunity to meet with a group of concerned individuals about schools struggling to meet the needs of their lower socioeconomic clientele. He quickly jotted down the contact information and decided to attend the first meeting. The note was placed inside his planner, and the research picked up where Mark had left off.

Mark opened up another book that indicated more recent and troubling trends: nearly 13 million American children live in families with incomes below the federal poverty level, which is $20,650 a year for a family of four. The number of children living in poverty has increased by 11% between 2000 and 2006, which translates into 1.2 million more children living in poverty in 2006 than in 2000. Research has consistently shown that, on average, families must maintain an income of about *twice the federal poverty level* to make ends meet. More than 28 million children in 2006—39% percent of all children living in the United States—were in low-income families or families identified as having four persons in the household and making no more than $41,000 (Douglas-Hall & Chau 2007).

For children whose parents face these ongoing financial challenges, living in poverty means that there is a greater likelihood of growing up amid conflict and stress. The struggle to make ends meet on a daily basis leaves little time and energy for the development of close, nurturing relationships between a parent and child. The emotional and physiological stresses related to repeated failures characteristic of impoverishment often leads to hopelessness and despair, beginning in the parents and transferring to the children. If there is a parent absent in the home for a variety of reasons, then the stresses are compounded as the single parent attempts to provide, nurture, and rear the children alone.

One's outlook on the future and on life in general translates into children who lack the tools necessary to achieve in school or to transition successfully into the workforce. Learning opportunities at home are limited as a result of a strained parent–child relationship, a lack of such home-based learning materials as books and computers, and an environment steeped with problems. When combined with limited access to decent child care and adequate nutrition, poor school performance and high school dropout rates are almost guaranteed. Thus, the result is a continuation of the generational poverty cycle (Miller & Weber 2004).

What strategies would it take to turn this cycle of generational poverty around? Would it be possible for Mark's students to actually engage in the classroom on a comparative standard against high-performing students, even within the same district? Would the meeting of concerned individuals help him as he searched for answers? He reasoned that even if he had to do it alone, the work could be accomplished and even further that it deserved to be accomplished; therefore, he set his mind to the task of restructuring Washington Elementary—one room at a time.

CONSTANCY IN THE MIDST OF CHANGE

It was obvious that Nancy loved teaching science at Barlow Middle School because she was beginning her 10th year there. During that time, she had experienced plenty of change: new principals, new assistant principals, new faculty and staff, and even a new district superintendent. Yet throughout all of this, Nancy found a constant in her life: her love of students. It did not matter to the class; all of her students knew they were loved while in that science classroom.

This year was no different. Nancy began in much the same way that she had begun so many other years. The first week was dedicated not to the curriculum but to a focused approach at learning each child, while understanding their backgrounds, their strengths, and their weaknesses. Nancy was a believer that if she understood her students, then she could reach them more effectively over the course of the year. And obviously, her approach was working because she maintained the highest scores on campus and the least amount of discipline problems.

Barlow Middle School was not situated in a predominant part of the city and was not considered one of the district's premier schools. In fact, if one investigated the makeup of Barlow, one would find a large percentage of African Americans and Hispanics, and an even larger percentage of free and reduced-price lunches being served. Nancy understood the socioeconomic and ethnic qualities of Barlow, yet she felt called into the school's family. Even though Nancy was Caucasian and middle class, she had a heart for underrepresented students and their families. She also believed in them and in their ability to perform on a competitive level with any other student in the district or the state. Her students were a compelling presence each year at the annual science fair, hosted by a neighboring community college. Several had been awarded ribbons and money for their excellence and creativity in many science strands. One student had proven her worth by graduating from high school and then college, all made possible by a scholarship won during a statewide science fair. What strategies did Nancy use in her classroom that encouraged such performance from her students, while three doors down, another teacher struggled with classroom management and student performance? Much of what is understood about human relationships stem from one word: respect.

One of her students named Tamisha recounted a story that occurred at a neighboring middle school where she attended the previous year. Tamisha's mom served as an aide in that school and verified the story to Nancy. Apparently, a student in the same grade as Tamisha had become a perpetual problem, even by the end of the first 9 weeks. He was always being referred to the principal's office because of misbehaving in the classrooms. When the principal had finally exhausted all of his behavior incentives, he was faced with three days' suspension.

On the first day of the young man's suspension, a teacher spotted him on campus roaming the halls. He was immediately taken to the office, where the principal sternly reminded him of his punishment. Since he lived in walking distance of the school, he was sent on his way. On the second day, a fellow student reported having seen him in the vicinity of the cafeteria. He was this time driven home by the school's counselor. On the third day, the principal saw him. He could not understand what was going on, why this young man would insist on breaking every rule to come back to school.

After a few moments, the principal called the young man into his office. This time, instead of being angry over the student's misbehaving, he was curious over his return to the middle school. The young man began to cry and explained that the meals that were served at this school were his only food. His mother had taken a third job to just pay the rent, and there was never enough money left over to provide food. He took his chances during his suspension just so he could have something to eat.

The principal determined that very day to rethink the school's standards. He allowed the child back into the classroom and called a faculty meeting for that very afternoon. As he explained the story to the faculty, he asked them to brainstorm possible strategies for this type of situation. That one act turned the entire community around. One after another, teachers, students, and parents began to see their school as something more than just a place to dispense knowledge. It became a place to dispense hope and care to all those in its area. Students grasped the concept of the golden rule and began to live in a manner that truly embodied the words.

As Nancy heard Tamisha and her mom tell the story, her eyes filled with tears. What had happened in our schools to cause the adults to lose touch with their students in such a way that this was not even known until the suspension had occurred? Would it have continued to go unnoticed unless this had happened? And now that it was known, would something be done to help the countless others facing the same predicament? Nancy tossed these and other questions around in her mind.

Before the end of the week, Nancy had talked with other teachers and had determined to begin a concerned citizens group to prevent such incidents from occurring again—at least in their area. One principal took the initiative and made informative flyers to be placed around area libraries and other public places. Another teacher volunteered to house the meeting at her home and provide refreshments. Now they waited to see who would show up.

A CULTURE OF CARE

Words have meaning, and unless that meaning is uncovered, then often the communication between two individuals can quickly turn into miscommunication. Therefore, as educators seek to understand what a culture of care may appear as in their school building, it becomes pertinent to define the words *culture* and *care*. For this particular usage, *culture* has been defined as the "systems of values, beliefs, and ways of knowing that guide communities of people in their daily lives" (Rothstein-Fisch & Trumbull 2008, p. 35). *Care* has been described as that which embodies empathy and emotion yet is demonstrated through an active engagement with someone.

Mark and Nancy carried with them a culture of care, in that their values, beliefs, and ways of knowing were manifest through this attitude of empathy toward other human beings—specifically, their students. Caring educators have the unique opportunity to reach out across any conceivable societal division and extend a helping hand to those in need. Through purposeful dialogue, deep reflection, and mindful inquiry, Mark and Nancy were able to realize that with the blended practice of caring and teaching, each could advance the learning of all children.

Valenzuela (1999) states, "If children do not know who they are or where they are going, then any road will get them there" (p. 269). Caring educators do not merely accept the "any road" approach to teaching. Instead, there remains a purpose much higher than merely scores on a test. The purpose to guide and instruct a life, even a life racked with poverty or neglect, becomes the caring educator's calling. Gould (2003) adds, "What can be more powerful than combining the virtue of a clear goal pursued relentlessly and without compromise, and the flexibility of a wide range of clever and distinct strategies for getting to the appointed place?" (p. 276).

Indeed, Mark and Nancy had determined within their souls that there is nothing more powerful than what Gould describes. Because of their passionate intensity of care for their students, both educators pursued a path of understanding and growth—not only during the summer months but continuing throughout the school year.

> **TIME TO REFLECT**
>
> What are your thoughts on care within the classroom? Do you share that intensity and passion about your students, so much so that you pursue professional opportunities to provide flexibility and creativity in the strategies used? If your passion has diminished over time, what might be done to reenergize your work? Brainstorm some possibilities with your colleagues, and examine if there might be a specific area where care injected into the learning experience could shift the outcome.

SIGNS OF HOPE

The school year had begun on a good note for Mark and Nancy. After being introduced at the first announced meeting, they both had found a wonderful support group while at the same time learning about sound, research-based strategies that worked in schools serving lower socioeconomic students and their families. Friendships had grown, and lessons had been learned. Both grew in their abilities to teach, as well as in their abilities to serve the community.

As the year progressed, Mark watched his students show signs of improvement in reading and language arts. He also saw them participating in the school's first science fair, with two of his students winning ribbons. There were also positive indicators of their social growth, as they understood the need for classroom rules and procedures. All in all, it had been a good year for the students and for Mark. He had learned so much about teaching and was already excited about returning next year. But the most important lesson was yet to come. It arrived in the form of an e-mail from a coworker at Washington Elementary during the latter part of the summer months. She informed him of the unexpected death of one of his students. Apparently, just a week before the tragedy, Michael had been caught trespassing onto a nearby apartment complex. He wanted to go swimming, and since his housing development did not have a pool, he found one not too far away. He had climbed the fence and upon seeing him, concerned neighbors reported him to the police. Nevertheless, Michael did not stop trying until he had successfully made it to the pool; unfortunately, he had never learned how to swim, and because of this, he drowned.

Mark could not believe that his young student, so full of life and adventure just a few weeks earlier, was now dead. Alone in the living room, Mark began to contemplate the news. He wondered about the impact he had upon Michael's short life and upon the lives of all the other students, and he realized that this learning community of which he was a part was much more than test scores, much more than just being a training ground for yet another learning strategy. These were flesh-and-blood human beings with all of the potential placed inside them that he had had placed inside himself. He would never look at a group of students the same way again.

REFERENCES

Caldas, S., & Bankston, C. (1997). Effect of school population: Socioeconomic status on individual academic achievement. *Journal of Educational Research*, 90(5), 269–277.

Coleman, J. (1966). *Equality of educational opportunity*. Washington, DC: Government Printing Office.

Crane, J. (1991). The epidemic theory of ghettoes and neighborhood effects on dropping out and teenage childbearing. *The American Journal of Sociology*, 96(5), 1226–1259.

Douglas-Hall, A., & Chau, M. (2007). Basic facts about low-income children, birth to age 18. National Center for Children in Poverty. Retrieved February 28, 2007, from http://www.nccp.org/publications/pub_762.html

Entwisle, D., Alexander, K., & Olson, L. (1997). *Children, schools and inequality*. Boulder: Westview Press.

Gould, S. J. (2003). *The hedgehog, the fox, and the magister's pox: Ending the false war between science and humanities.* New York: Harmony.

Jencks, C. (1972). The Coleman Report and conventional wisdom. In F. Mosteller & D. Moynihan (Eds.), *On equality of educational opportunity* (pp. 69–115). New York: Vintage Books.

Mayer, S. (1991). How much does a high school's racial and socioeconomic mix affect graduation rates and teenage fertility rates? In C. Jencks & P. Peterson (Eds.), *The urban underclass* (pp. 321–341). Washington, DC: Brookings Institution.

Miller, K. K., & Weber, B. A. (2004). Persistent poverty and place: How do persistent poverty dynamics and demographics vary across the rural–urban continuum? Southern Rural Development Center, Oregon State University. Retrieved January 12, 2008, from http://srdc.msstate.edu/measuring/series/miller_weber.pdf.

National Center for Educational Statistics. (1999). *National assessment for educational progress (NAEP): Report card for the nation and states.* Washington, DC: U.S. Department of Education.

Rothstein-Fisch, C., & Trumbull, E. (2008). *Managing diverse classrooms: How to build on students' cultural strengths.* Alexandria, VA: Association for Supervision and Curriculum Development.

Rumberger, R., & Willms, D. (1992). The impact of racial and ethnic segregation on the achievement gap in California high schools. *Educational Evaluation and Policy Analysis, 14*(4), 377–396.

Valenzuela, A. (1999). *Subtractive schooling: U.S.–Mexican youth and the politics of caring.* Albany: State University of New York Press.

7

THE SCIENCE OF LEARNING

Ann Guilbert

The important thing is not to stop questioning. Curiosity has its own reason for existing.

—Albert Einstein

Many have learned science in school through traditional methods, such as reading chapters in a textbook and finding conclusions of what scientists have learned in previous decades. Knowing science meant knowing the scientific terms at the end of the chapter and reciting the facts about the discoveries of those who were exploring the natural world. We were taught the formulaic process known as the scientific method, although we never did anything with it. There was discussion of how hypotheses could be derived and tested but tests, if conducted at all, were only conducted by teacher demonstration. The emphasis on the scientific method was to show how scientists, not students, determined *how* and *what* they needed or wanted to know of the ways the world works (National Academy Press [NAP] 2005).

Shortly after 1957, when the Russians beat the United States into space, there was an outcry that focused funding and research on school science and how it should be taught. What followed was the production of foolproof teacher kits designed to provide children with hands-on experiences, the kind that even teachers could not mess up. Within a decade, those encouraging hands-on science experiences for children over desk experiences came to the conclusion that just providing materials in a classroom did not change how students were learning science. Subsequently, over the following 3 decades, much effort has been put into training teachers to create a learning environment that does not remove the student from an authentic discovery experience but inserts the student into a genuine opportunity to question and discover (Zemelman, Daniels, & Hyde 2005).

In addition to the attention put on teacher preparation and professional development, such associations as the American Association for the Advancement of Science (AAAS), the National Research Council (NRC), and the National Science Teachers Association (NSTA) sought to create documents that clearly defined a national vision for scientific literacy (AAAS 1989; NRC 1996, 2000). Effective science programs were outlined by identifying concepts that schools should be teaching, instructional strategies that supported student achievement, assessment that guided learning experiences, and essential skills that should be developed in scientifically literate persons. At the same time this image of science literacy was being created, the learning environment was being influenced and shaped by research on how the brain works and how people learn (NAP 2005). Designers of teacher preparation programs in science have used what researchers discovered to develop programs that train teachers of science in strategies that can allow students to experience authentic science and construct a learning environment based on the evidence of cognitive science (Kellough & Kellough 2008).

> **TIME TO REFLECT**
>
> The professional organizations for science call for teachers to develop classroom instruction that includes hands-on inquiry, questioning that leads students to make connections about major concepts, and assessment to ensure students understand rather than just memorize. What are the components of the program in your subject area that are called for by your professional organization? What instructional strategies would you use to make sure that you have a research-based program in your school?

CURIOSITY AND PROBLEM SOLVING

Zemelman, Daniels, and Hyde (2005) examined documents released by AAAS, NSTA, and NRC and determined qualities of best practice that should be present in science classrooms across the nation. This chapter focuses on a young teacher who, although she was in her first year of teaching, created a learning environment that included many of those qualities of best practice and ultimately established the foundation for her students to score in the highest percentiles on the state and national exams in science.

Teachers who teach science should build on students' curiosity about the natural world and provide opportunities for them to conduct inquiry to answer their own questions (Zemelman et al. 2005). There are countless phenomena that teachers can use to harness the innate curiosity of students and develop their passion for exploring. Meredith is one of those teachers who place unleashing her students' curiosity at the heart of her instruction. She consistently presents opportunities in her classroom for students to pursue their own interests and develop that natural curiosity.

In a visit one day, Meredith spoke with passion about how she used students' inquisitive nature to guide her: "I honestly think that the teaching needs to come from the students and not necessarily always from me. I'm not saying that I shouldn't be teaching them, but I think they can teach from doing, from each other and from themselves." She wanted them to be curious and to be able to ask questions. She wanted them to be able to solve problems and understand the very nature of science. Her enthusiasm and own inquisitive nature boosted the students' desire to investigate and find the answers to questions.

During another visit in her classroom, she had students working on several different projects. One pair of boys was working but had finished early. When they told her they were done she quickly designed an extension to what they were doing. To challenge them beyond her objective for their learning that day, she handed them an actual thermometer that did not have any numbers on it and asked them to come up with a way to put numbers on it. She asked them how they would measure where zero should be and how they could know where the other numbers should be located. The students discussed and gathered ideas for a while and then began to work. They went outside and brought in a container of snow. They put the thermometer in the container of snow and marked a line when the alcohol had ceased to move downward. Meredith reflected, "I didn't give them that. I mean, they had to do some thinking on their own. So that's how I'm trying to see what they know and I know that they are not just playing but analyzing and problem solving."

She went on to explain that she is trying to broaden their scope of thinking by having them think of all the different ways that they can measure things. She talked of the frustration that she feels when she sees them stopping because they do not want to go beyond a certain level of thinking and questioning: "They do a problem and they are done. They don't want to think about any other additional ideas. I am constantly asking, 'What would happen if . . .' or 'Have you tried this?'"

SELF-SUFFICIENCY

Zemelman and colleagues (2005) point out that teachers are to help their students become increasingly self-directed learners. Teachers should help students become less dependent on them for guidance and increasingly self-reliant during the school year and over many years. Students need to become more metacognitive, more able to monitor their own processes of inquiry. They must learn how to recognize when they do not understand and should seek more information. They need to realize when they should ask questions, such as, "What evidence would convince me that these explanations are probably true?"

Meredith sees what happens in her classroom in this light. She focuses everyday on reaching her goals of creating self-sufficient learners as well as developing critical thinkers. She always expresses the importance of students' ability to problem solve and think things through. She never indicates that these are skills that will be used on the test in the spring but holds onto the idea that if she can challenge them to think and problem solve, then she can change the level of success they will have in life: "I don't think about what they will be like as middle school students. I am constantly developing skills and content they will need as college students. That is how they will pass the test they have this year and in life."

Meredith expresses frustration when students quit thinking or try to be dependent on her for the answers. She wants them to know what to do when they get stuck on something. She wants them to figure out how they can get themselves going again. In each class she models questions they can ask themselves to go beyond the point of being stuck: "Can I just skip to the next problem? Or maybe it's just getting up and looking in another book, but I want *them* to do it! That is a big thing for me, self-sufficiency in my class. I want them so independent in their learning that if a sub walked in on any day and didn't know what they were doing, the students would just automatically get out their work and get going."

Afterward, Meredith shared an experience the students had in class. They were discussing and debating about matter and what things were or were not matter. Some of the students were confident about the decisions they had made in the discussion during the lesson. These students were adamant about their definition. They were able to provide evidence to support their idea, and when they had questions about things, they were not afraid to ask the question, "How can we find out?"

THE ART AND HEART OF QUESTIONING

Meredith describes a good learner as someone who is always questioning: "Questioning the textbooks or the things the teacher has said—not in a disrespectful way but in a manner such as 'Show me or prove this' or 'Show me what you are talking about.' I always want them to point out contradictions or things that don't seem to make sense."

Not all of Meredith's students will become scientists, but the design of her classroom has fostered in all of her students the awareness of science as a dynamic, creative interplay of questions and evidence, data and ideas, predictions and explanations. Each of her students experiences the excitement of the search for answers and ways to put pieces of information together to make sense of the world they are a part of. Meredith's students are immersed in a learning environment that has enormous power to invite them to a state of inquisitiveness and the pursuit of the unanswered question.

TIME TO REFLECT

You are a new science teacher in grades 5–8. The principal comes to visit your room to conduct an observation. You have the students working on various investigations. Students are all around the room, gathering materials, asking each other questions, talking to you about their work, and writing down ideas that come as they explore. You are excited that he has come when the students are so engaged. After a few minutes the principal gets up from his seat, moves to the door and says, "I'll come back when you are teaching." When you have the opportunity to talk to him about his reaction to what he saw, what rationale would you give for the type of classroom you designed? Why should a teacher have a research base for every decision he or she makes in the classroom? Write down your vision for how the classroom should be designed in your subject area. Develop a research-based rationale for including each aspect of instruction.

Students in most science classrooms do not have the opportunity to ask and pursue their own questions. Meredith knows that for students to develop the ability to ask questions, they must practice doing so. There are times when she provides the question for them and other times when they develop their own questions. Sometimes the questions are answered individually; sometimes they are answered based on a group who is interested in finding out about one idea; and sometimes they are given the answer to the question with developmentally appropriate explanations. Some of the time, the lesson that Meredith designs causes students to develop questions that extend their own personal learning.

Not only does Meredith use questions to engross and motivate students, but she also uses them to assess how students are making connections from the experiences they are having in the classroom to the content that she wants them to learn. She has seen that good questions help teachers identify students' misconceptions, and they help students work through their uncertainties or expand their ideas (Enger & Yager 2001).

Research indicates that teachers who use the inquiry approach in their science classrooms should stay focused on ensuring students understand the concepts (Zemelman et al. 2005). Meredith is continually interacting with students, discussing their investigations and the data they collect. She uses the interactions as a means of determining whether students are drawing conclusions about the underlying principle or if they are able to use what they learn to connect to new knowledge. For Meredith, the conversations that ensue between herself and her students are compelling evidence of students' understanding of the content or process that they are learning. When asked how she tells if students are learning what she wants them to, Meredith's response is:

> By their ability to answer questions and their ability to ask questions, being able to do something with what they have learned. They may be able to sit there and do all of these experiments, but they may not be able to tell me anything that they've learned. When they journal I have them talk about the things that they've learned. I also have them draw illustrations on the chalkboard. Many times I'll ask them to come to the board and show me what they are thinking about. That really helps me to see whether they have an understanding of what we're doing. Then I'll ask them to show me on material that they're working with right then and there. Boy, it is clear evidence!

It is most exciting to Meredith when students can take something from several experiences and apply it to a new situation. An example she gives of such an experience was during a lesson when students were working on an activity to enhance their measurement skills. They were working with different ice shapes and determining various aspects of measurement. During one of her interactions with the students, a boy mentioned something that she had written on the board about consistency of variables being compared. She asked him to explain a bit further about what he thought was going to happen based on consistency or inconsistency of the variable and the experimental factor. The student brought to her attention that the ice cubes had been out all day in the coolers and that they probably were not all the same size by the time the class period was over. She asked him what he was going to do when the ice cubes were not the same size. He told her about the things he had done at each of the stations and the tests he had run on the ice at each of the other tables. Based on his conclusions at each of the other areas and information that he had gathered from various investigations they had done throughout the year, he had put together a way to test and measure with the added variable of melting. Meredith explains, "So he was really able to take a lot of different things that we had done throughout the year and apply them to a new situation, and *new* is the key word there because he had not seen what he was talking about. This indicated to me that he had a great deal of understanding about what was going on."

> **TIME TO REFLECT**
>
> Think about how you determine if students meet the learning objective after instruction. What behaviors would you look for in students who communicate that they have an understanding of the concept you are teaching? Give an example of how you can assess to see if students got it. Choose a concept from your subject area, and give an example of how to modify a lesson to enrich or reteach a concept.

Just as teachers in reading classes are focused on developing literacy skills in their students, students in science classrooms should be improving the skills that enhance their scientific literacy. Teachers have to design instruction so that students have classrooms that encourage mastery of scientific knowledge and processes while they use logic and reasoning to draw conclusions and make connections. Instructional design that supports scientific literacy engages students in scientific questions, provides opportunities for students to explore those questions, requires students to interpret data and create explanations, and allows them to evaluate what they have learned in the light of other knowledge.

Additional instructional methods commonly used in all classrooms that support scientific thinking are those found in Marzano, Pickering, and Pollock's (2001) meta-analysis of the research in *Classroom Instruction That Works*. A student's scientific literacy is enhanced by such strategies as identifying similarities and differences; summarizing and note taking; using nonlinguistic representations; participating in cooperative learning; setting objectives and providing feedback; generating and testing hypotheses; and using questioning, cues, and advance organizers. Teachers in teacher preparations programs, alternative certification programs, or in their own classrooms everyday should create lessons to utilize these methods and raise the level of student thinking in every subject area. Such cognitive challenges, as Meredith stated, raise the level of a student's chances to be successful on the test and in life.

The most effective science teachers design lessons around questions that students ask. They do not hesitate to ask many questions during their lessons. Compared to less effective teachers, these teachers pose more questions and ask more follow-up questions with higher cognitive demand (Krueger & Sutton 2001; NRC 1996, 2000). Students in these classrooms are expected to share ideas with others in order to clarify their thinking.

Many science educators have argued fervently against the high-stakes tests in place at both the state and national levels. However, a teacher should not hesitate to create a classroom based on the best practices of actively engaging students in authentic science experiences; encouraging problem solving and questioning; and cultivating a self-sufficient, conceptual learner. Students in classrooms that have these components perform well on both knowledge and process parts of state and national assessments.

REFERENCES

American Association for the Advancement of Science. (1989). *Science for all Americans: A project 2061 report on literacy goals in science, mathematics, and technology.* Washington, DC: American Association for the Advancement of Science.

Enger, S., & Yager, R. (2001). *Assessing student understanding in science.* Thousand Oaks, CA: Corwin Press.

Kellough, R., & Kellough, N. (2008). *Teaching young adolescents: A guide to methods and resources.* 5th ed. Columbus, OH: Prentice Hall.

Krueger, A., & Sutton, J. (Eds.). (2001). *EDThoughts: What we know about science teaching and learning.* Aurora, CO: Mid-Continent Research for Education and Learning.

Marzano, R., Pickering, D., & Pollock, J. (2001). *Classroom instruction that works.* Alexandria, VA: Association for Supervision and Curriculum Development.

National Academy Press. (2005). *How people learn.* Washington, DC: National Academy Press.

National Research Council. (1996). *National science education standards.* Washington, DC: National Academy Press.

National Research Council. (2000). *Inquiry and the national science education standards: A guide for teaching and learning.* Washington, DC: National Academy Press.

Zemelman, S., Daniels, H., & Hyde, A. (2005). *Best practice: Today's standards for teaching and learning in America's schools.* Portsmouth, NH: Heinemann.

8

WHEN ALL IS SAID AND DONE

Sherry Durham

A child's life is like a piece of paper on which every passerby leaves a mark.

—Chinese proverb

THE EXPERIENCE OF TIME

It is amazing the impact a teacher can have on the life of a student. Even more amazing is the impact one student may have on the life of a teacher and his or her praxis in the classroom as well. In the most difficult of situations, a ray of hope or instruction manual for a successful year can often be located inside the four walls that make up a school classroom.

All a teacher needs to do to locate the answer to some of the most profound and challenging situations is take time to evaluate the actions in the classroom (students and teacher), think through the process of what makes for an environment conducive for learning, and begin to create that environment with the teacher in control and totally focused on the act and art of instruction while building relationships fairly. Classroom management and conscious actions to address student behavior and motivation through learning opportunities will make a great difference in the school day of children and teachers. Stopping to make policies for classroom behavior and setting expectations through collaboration is one step that can make the learning journey more meaningful.

THE WISDOM OF YEARS

Carol officially qualified for retirement after teaching 27 years, but she loves her work and always looked forward to another year of students excitedly waiting to learn more about the world around them. She is a master teacher in every sense of the word. The state accountability tests consistently provide necessary documentation that her students score above the state average in reading and math. Recognized as a mentor to new teachers, Carol is also regarded as one of the strongest reading teachers in the district.

However, this school year did not begin as previous years had. The discipline in her 3rd-grade classroom proved extremely difficult to maintain, and she found herself sending more and more students to the principal's office. Carol used the traditional methods, such as phoning parents and establishing classroom rules and consequences, but to no avail.

Carol's campus remained focused on practice for accountability testing. There were timelines and benchmarks in place that provided an organized method of teacher monitoring by administrators because the campus had received the "acceptable" score 1 year earlier, breaking their history of receiving "recognition." Carol simply did not have enough time to deal with all of the behavior issues arising in her class while maintaining her assurance of teaching the targeted expectations. Because of the added pressure, Carol quickly became frustrated and felt as if she needed to get out of the education business altogether.

> **TIME TO REFLECT**
>
> Have you ever found yourself in a situation that left you feeling overwhelmed and frustrated? What led you to that place of frustration? How did you find your way out?

Throughout this battle for control of the classroom, there was one student who seemed to always find himself in the middle of any disruption. Edwin constantly roamed about the classroom and seldom found his seat; he was rude and loud and typically behaved as a bully to the other students. From time to time, items would be missing, and Edwin's name would quickly surface as the suspected perpetrator. Carol knew he was taking other students' belongings but failed to catch him in the act. She wanted to converse with the child, but unfortunately, there was not enough time in the day to effectively teach and monitor misbehaving students. Carol simply had her hands full.

Edwin's all-consuming desire to gain Carol's attention stemmed from the fact that he was living with his grandmother while occasionally seeing his mother and rarely seeing his father. Carol understood Edwin's need to be accepted and loved, so she attempted to develop a relationship with the grandmother through notes and phone calls. However, Grandma Evelyn worked two jobs and had not planned on having to raise children again. She was also faced with the fact that Edwin was more than she could handle, so Grandma Evelyn concluded that Carol was on her own in dealing with Edwin's behavior at school.

Carol's sense of overwhelming discouragement continued to mount, as her school district adopted the philosophy of teaching in which high-quality lessons would now include differentiation of student learning. Not only was discipline out of control, but expectations for students to meet or surpass state guidelines on the yearly accountability test were at an all-time high, and a new philosophy of instruction monitored with unannounced drop-in visits by the principal were bearing down on Carol with a vengeance.

At her wit's end, Carol was forced to make a decision: save the school's reputation for excellence in testing or save the child. She opted for the student. Carol distinctly remembers the turning point in her career when, as she was driving to school, she heard a radio commentator speak about finding purpose in life. Carol pulled the car over to the side of the road and began to sob. The words that flowed from her car speakers tugged at her heart, and she found hope as the stranger spoke about the role each individual plays in the scheme of humanity and that all have a purpose for being where they are; each must simply look for it and understand.

It was at that moment that Carol became a believer: she believed that she could make a difference for Edwin, as well as the rest of her students. Her focus had merely been on the instructional outcome instead of the journey. Carol vowed in her car that morning to take each day and do with it what she could. Her students, even Edwin, needed her, and she needed them; after all, she was their teacher.

> **TIME TO REFLECT**
>
> What is your purpose for being in the classroom? Has your purpose changed from your first year as a teacher to now? How has that purpose changed? Describe the journey that you have experienced since becoming an educator.

Returning on Monday, Carol determined to first have a discussion with her students. They talked about what was important in the classroom and the role that student behavior plays in learning, and Carol provided the students an opportunity to see the correct behavior modeled. The classmates agreed upon the need to respect others and their property, to use their quiet voices when talking, and finally to listen when the teacher spoke. A classroom declaration of behavior was created, and each student signed his or her name—just as they did with the Declaration of Independence. The document was then posted on the front wall as a reminder to each person.

Carol then requested a meeting with her principal and began to explain her plan of action, placing top priority on each child and then on the benchmark scores. He hesitantly agreed but reminded her about the mandates placed upon each member of the school by district officials.

> **TIME TO REFLECT**
>
> Have you ever felt torn between district testing requirements and the individuality of your students? What was the outcome of this internal turmoil? Which group ultimately won your complete attention?

During the next few weeks, instruction time was filled with choral readings, reader's theaters, and art projects—all grounded in the latest learning strategies' research. Instead of filling the time with worksheets and timed test preparation material, her students began to show huge gains from Carol's use of higher-order thinking skills, questioning strategies, conversational learning, and differentiated learning experiences—even Edwin.

Carol's turning point made all the difference in her teaching career—both for her and her students. She continued to look for opportunities to positively impact each child in her classroom, not only in the area of testing competence, but also in the areas related to their social, emotional, and mental competence. Just as Carol found purpose in life through hearing the radio commentator's words, so do her students hear that they have a purpose, too. And when all has been said and done, Carol hopes that their purpose also instills within each one a deep sense of calling.

IMPLICATIONS OF RELATIONSHIPS

Darlene treated herself to a manicure occasionally as a special treat. Regardless of the infrequency of her visits to the salon, each time she walked in the door, she was treated as if she were royalty. The owners of the establishment would rush to give her a hug and tell her how highly she was held in regard by their family. If she encountered them in the grocery store or at the local discount store, the reaction was the same. What caused this ordinary-looking school teacher to have this impact on people? A relationship was established when she taught the son of immigrants from Vietnam.

Tu was a 3rd-grader when his parents moved to a small town in Texas. As a second-language learner, it was difficult for him to keep up with his peers. He was much smaller in stature than his classmates and thus a target for bullying and teasing. By all accounts, this child should have experienced a miserable 3rd-grade year, but with Mrs. Mosley as his teacher, his best year ever in public schools in America was 3rd grade.

She worked with him before school to allow him a preview of the content she was teaching for the day. Phone calls and parent meetings offered a link between school and home to keep parents informed of school events and Tu's academic progress. Mrs. Mosley also offered opportunities for her class to learn more about Vietnam and Tu's culture, often allowing him to be the guest speaker, sharing his knowledge and helping him to be seen as an expert instead of an outsider. No teasing or bullying was allowed as a general rule, but Mrs. Mosley made an intense effort to offer opportunities for building relationships of acceptance and support within her class.

The tone set for the acceptance of a student from a different culture was set by the teacher. Mrs. Mosley offered kindness and the desire to support this student through several avenues, such as involving parents and extra time not only for tutorials but for preteaching segments to facilitate deeper understanding for the

> **TIME TO REFLECT**
>
> There are many students entering classrooms as English-language learners. How do you address their needs for an invitational classroom setting? What steps do you take to involve their parents in the learning process?

content at first presentation. These practices did not require intense staff development or deep-pocket funding. These were the actions of a teacher creating a learning environment to offer each student, regardless of background or ability, the chance to learn and become a member of a community of learners. If her entire focus had been whether Tu was going to pass the state accountability tests, she would have bombarded him with practice worksheets and spent hours offering him more practice time to pass the tests. Instead she offered him significant instruction in a meaningful way; oral language was strengthened and vocabulary reinforced through authentic practices with his peers.

Engaging lessons offer all students relevant learning experiences. Sadly, many classrooms operate in the manner described by Silver, Strong, and Perini (2000) as those "with the premium placed on content coverage and independent seatwork at the expense of diverse and engaging learning opportunities" (p. 46). This is the result of pressures for teachers to cover the content, disregarding thoughts of teaching for deeper understanding or offering opportunities for critical thinking to take place.

> **TIME TO REFLECT**
>
> What is taking place in your classroom? How do you offer high-quality instruction and opportunities for learning balanced with preparing students to be successful on accountability tests? Are there compromises to be made? Are there winners and losers in the outcome?

WHAT MATTERS MOST

Teachers' roles are becoming increasingly important in the lives of their students. Too often they become the moral compass for these children, with parents absent from the home due to work schedules, divorce, imprisonment, and sometimes rampant neglect and ignorance. According to Popkewitz (1998), "What began as civic responsibility was transformed into a pastoral power to rescue the child. The moral responsibility of schooling is to govern the soul, inner beliefs, feelings, and sensitivities that generate actions" (p. 49).

Federal and state accountability testing dictating classroom practice has become rampant with little regard for developing the whole student. Popkewitz (1998) further tells us, "Classrooms are organized to bring forth something unrealized—that is, a capacity or a potential that is presumed to lie within the individual that is not yet visible" (p. 44). A teacher unlocks the potential within each student and allows the process of becoming to happen. The heart and mind of each child is molded by the teacher's input and actions on a daily basis, not only as an academic leader of the classroom, but also as the individual leading the child in developing a love for learning and respect for his or her fellow classmates.

TIME TO REFLECT

What have you recently done through your classroom practice that provides a sense of value and regard to your students? How do you balance the requirements of federal, state, and district accountability expectations with individualized student instruction?

Looking into the classrooms of today, one often is met with a view clouded by the looming accountability testing preparation. Schlechty

(2002) speaks to the idea and value of accountability in classrooms, especially with regard for states that currently have student assessment standards in place: "The idea that standards are important to learning is certainly not lost on teachers . . . however [for standards] to motivate, they must have meaning and perceived value to those to whom they are being applied" (p. 86). Teachers must involve all students in the learning process if authentic student success is to be our goal.

Students should be asked to acknowledge areas of interest to them, implement an integration of higher-order thinking opportunities with real-life experiences, and develop a practice of unwavering devotion to reaching a deeper level of engagement. This cannot occur alone. It is only with the teacher modeling, motivating, and mentoring each through this process that true accountability for learning takes place, not for the tests, but in spite of the testing requirements. Therefore, we must be reminded, "It proceeds from the simple question: what is it that students care about that could be built into the tasks students are assigned that would make it more likely the students would become engaged and invest great effort in the task? The primary job of the teacher is to work out answers to this question every day" (Schlechty 2002, p. 88). Teachers who view these as colearning situations involving the students as well as themselves design an environment where all parties are involved in authentic inquiry and exploration. Teacher relationships with parents and students command great power. These bonds of support and care are necessary to facilitate the development of students into individuals capable of building future relationships such as they have experienced.

To truly make a difference for the future, teachers must not only address academic needs and strategic bars of learning held for accountability excellence but also daily measure their practice against the bar for molding good citizens with character and integrity for generations to follow.

REFERENCES

Popkewitz, T. S. (1998). *Struggling for the soul: The politics of schooling and the construction of the teacher.* New York: Teachers College Press.

Schlechty, P. C. (2002). *Working on the work: An action plan for teachers, principals, and superintendents.* San Francisco: Jossey-Bass.

Silver, H. F., Strong, R. W., & Perini, M. J. (2000). *So each may learn: Integrating learning styles and multiple intelligences.* Alexandria, VA: Association for Supervision and Curriculum Development.

9

RIF: REDUCTION IN FORCE OR REALIZATION IN THE FUTURE

Terri Hebert

If you will call your troubles experiences, and remember that every experience develops some latent force within you, you will grow vigorous and happy, however adverse your circumstances may seem to be.

—John R. Miller

Many school districts find themselves entering uncharted waters, as financial crises loom just ahead of the bend, and many school boards and superintendents find themselves making difficult decisions pertaining to their employees. As the words leave their leaders' mouths and enter into the ears of waiting faculty and staff, the term *RIF* (reduction in force) suddenly takes on an ominous meaning for themselves and their family members. Even though there are numerous messages that accompany the RIFing, it still leaves many without jobs, without a paycheck, and without security. In essence, everything promised has been taken away, and one is left to wonder what happened.

This is the story of one such district's response to its community's declaration of disproportionate spending, especially among the top-ranking school employees found within the central office. But more importantly, it is the age-old story of hope among the perceived ruins of a job that ended much too soon.

ANOTHER TIME AND ANOTHER PLACE

Several years ago there was a place filled with the anticipation of positive change. One individual was awaiting her chance at a job interview that promised hope and interest to all involved in this new direction. Maribeth waited in her car outside of the school district's administration building. She was looking over some last-minute material that might give her the words necessary to impress the interview team poised inside. As the second hand approached the time that Maribeth would step from the car and enter the double glass doors, she quickly breathed a prayer and pulled on the handle. This was her moment and she knew it.

The group of approximately 10 individuals consisting of teachers, administrators, and central office staff welcomed Maribeth into the seemingly small room. The light was dimmed, attempting to make for a cozy environment, yet it provided what seemed like an interrogation chamber instead. The head of the committee, as well as the director of curriculum and instruction—Mrs. Tillman—welcomed Maribeth and began the introductions. Maribeth looked into the eyes of each person and realized that they had had a long procession of interviews preceding hers. Nevertheless, Maribeth wanted to meet their eyes with a twinkle and a smile, as if she was the first person on the list.

The task of the committee was to hire the most qualified person for the science coordinator's position, which covered grades K–12. The district was the largest in the eastern part of the state and, because of this, had seen its share of ups and downs related to high-stakes testing and the scores that it produced. The superintendent was attempting to fill positions with the most qualified individuals to assist teachers in the preparation of the tests and to provide support structures for the teachers in their content areas. Thus, the science coordinator's position had been created to do just that. The questions were systematically asked of Maribeth, and her responses were appropriate. Before she knew it, the interview was over, and she was being led from the room to the outer lobby. It was here that Mrs. Tillman told her that someone would be in touch later that week to announce the group's decision.

As Maribeth drove home, she reflected on the events—all of them—and wondered if she had demonstrated enough to prove her capability and worth. Because it was afternoon, Maribeth did not return to school but drove home. She busied herself with the normal routine, glancing through the mail, cooking dinner, and the like. Nevertheless, her mind was entirely focused on that interview and the possibilities that lay ahead if the job became hers.

As she was watching television and talking with her children, the phone rang. Maribeth glanced at her watch and noticed that it was almost 9:00. She answered the phone, not really sure who was on the other end. The voice identified itself as one being from the interview committee, Mrs. Thompson. She had been given the task of calling to reveal the committee's decision and to ask if Maribeth was interested in taking the science coordinator's job. It was all that Maribeth could do to contain herself during that exchange on the phone. As soon as she had placed the receiver back where it belonged, she let out a loud scream of excitement. She could not believe that she had been offered and had accepted the position. It was a dream that had come true.

WELCOME TO THE CENTRAL OFFICE!

As Maribeth began her tenure as science coordinator, she found that she had entered into a steep learning curve. There were many things that she never understood about being a central office administrator, one of which was the distinct line that had invisibly been constructed, separating her from the teaching community. She couldn't remember the exact moment when the line was drawn and who had drawn it, but nevertheless, the line was definitely there, and it was difficult for Maribeth to navigate once-familiar territory.

Maribeth's first assignment as science coordinator was to introduce the new curriculum to all teacher groups during the in-service training opportunities given prior to the new school year. Maribeth had worked with these teachers during the previous year when they provided input and suggestions about the work that had been done. The overall feeling was not positive because many teachers felt that the curriculum constricted their autonomy levels. They understood the need for curriculum frameworks developed by the state department in conjunction with the national standards. However, for the district to step into the interpretation of those frameworks and mandate that each teacher follow a carefully constructed, month-by-month guideline of topics that would be taught and then tested, it proved too much for many of the district's science teachers. Now it was Maribeth's duty to introduce the completed work and pass out each teacher's copy of the district's science curriculum. Needless to say, she was met with overwhelming distrust and negativity.

At the conclusion of the in-service meeting, Maribeth returned to her office. She sat down and began to sob. What had she done? How had this happened to her? This was to be her dream job, and yet, it had turned into a nightmare. How could her colleagues—her friends—turn on her so quickly when in fact she was one of them just two months earlier? Maribeth tried to reflect on the incident and to learn from it, with the intention of performing at a higher level the next time she presented to the teachers.

However, it became apparent to Maribeth that she would not have the time needed to reflect upon past performances. Instead, assignments were thrown at her as fast as someone throwing darts at a dart board. She was required to devote more and more time to the small things and less time to major issues. The central office staff members moved from one item to another in a frenzy, and everyone soon began to feel overwhelmed by the enormity of the job.

As each new task was met with a determination to please Mrs. Tillman, it seemed that the work silently pulled her further and further away from those she was hired to assist. Maribeth rarely had time to spend on campuses and even less time to spend talking with teachers about their concerns and their desires. Somewhere along the way, Maribeth had left behind her focus of the classroom and the students. The job became the focus, with seemingly endless tasks filling up the day.

Time passed quickly, and soon Maribeth marked the end of her second year on the job. There were some gains to be reported, such as the creation of a vertical team approach among science teachers and a focused effort on the utilization of informal science educators in the community to provide content-specific professional development. But there were many other issues that lay dormant as Maribeth struggled with the direction to move. Many involved issues related to the curriculum and its standardized assessment procedures.

TIME TO REFLECT

As an educator, have you felt the pull of the small, minute tasks that eat away at your time and pull you from your intended focus? If so, what have you done to maintain that focus? What have your administrators done to help in maintaining your focus, which is found in teaching and learning? What suggestions might you give to help someone else in this area of time management?

DISTRICT CHANGES ON THE HORIZON

During the course of Maribeth's time at the central office, the community had failed to pass a bond proposal that would provide updated facilities for many of its students. It was clearly understood that the district needed such updates, but many community members felt that the district had not done an outstanding job maintaining the facilities currently in place. Therefore, they refused to provide additional money until there was some type of accountability in place for the money already provided.

One superintendent left, and another was hired to take his place. There was much uneasiness with the transfer of power, especially at the central office. Talk filtered through the ranks of possible staffing changes, especially in the curriculum and instruction department. Maribeth felt that her position was secure, especially because a new state testing initiative was in progress that included science benchmarks. How could a district release a science coordinator if new science tests were being implemented? There would definitely need to be someone in place who could assist the teachers as they worked to prepare their students.

However, by the fifth month of the new superintendent's tenure, invitations had been sent out to all central office personnel that each person would visit with Dr. Monroe about his or her job. The tension mounted as the days approached for the visits. Maribeth wasn't quite sure what to make of all of this. Several of the senior members of the central office expressed their recollection of something like this happening many years earlier. Their thinking was that this amounted to the school board's attempt to diminish the negative outcries from the community, while at the same time to push forward a second try at another bond proposal election.

As Maribeth waited once again, she reflected on the speedy 2 years at the central office. What would she say to Dr. Monroe about her job, about the results that she had seen, and about the challenges that still remained? She knew that every word was critical and must be carefully chosen to prove her worth.

The interview proved uneventful. It seemed that nothing of value came out of the meeting; nothing of worth was really discussed. Maribeth did hear that a survey had been given to district principals, and questions related to each coordinator's performance on their particular campus. She was never given an opportunity to examine each document, to learn of their comments, and to make the necessary adjustments. Shortly before spring break, news spread of the 20 cuts that would be made—all of which were found within the central office.

Maribeth was devastated at the news. How could this be? This was her dream job. This was her calling. Yet, she now lived with the fact that at the end of the school year, her job would be no more. The teachers would be without a science coordinator. The district would be without a voice from the science community. And in the fall of the next school year, science tests would be given. There was no sense to be made of the announcement, only shock.

Money seemed to be the driving force behind all of the changes. The community demanded accountability from the district as to how their money had been spent in years past, and they wanted a promise of security if more money was given in a future bond election. The school district seemed driven to cut back the funds required to maintain a staff at the central office in hopes of proving to the community its fiscal responsibility, and the teachers and students wished for more money to flow into the schools so that they could purchase needed equipment for the classrooms. The quick-fix answer was found within the school's right to reduce its workers if budgetary constraints found it necessary to do so.

The days and weeks moved at a snail's pace. Maribeth dreaded coming to the office. There were constant reminders of those who were leaving, as well as those who were asked to stay. People talked of relocation within the building, and individuals would come by and look at offices to determine if that was the one they wanted. The work with the teachers also came to a standstill, as everyone knew that there was no more authority in the position of science coordinator. It was merely a matter of time before change would bring about something new. And the teachers waited, too, for what that something might be. Maribeth's focus now was on securing a job for the fall.

The pain was too immense to talk about with friends and family. There was a sense of embarrassment at the fact that Maribeth's job was ceasing and also a sense of failure because she had failed to perform to a level worthy of continuation. This was what was implied by the superintendent when he revealed the survey results. Maribeth had never failed at a position before. In fact, she had always prided herself in the fact that a job was done well.

What was she to do and where was she to go? And what would happen to the teachers and students? Probably the most definitive question was this: Would the district even miss her presence? These questions haunted her every moment.

TIME TO REFLECT

Have you experienced a reduction in force at your school district? If so, did it directly impact you? How was it handled by the administrators and school board members? What did you learn from the experience?

THE TIE THAT BINDS: FINANCES AND ACHIEVEMENT

All across the United States, standards-based reform movements are underway in hopes of raising the level of student achievement. NCLB ushered in a new wave of response by the federal government as they seek to provide aid in reaching this goal, especially for children in poverty and for those facing some form of disability or language disparity. Arkansas happens to be one of a number of states (e.g., Arizona, Delaware, Georgia, North Carolina, and Wyoming) that are currently facing court mandates to level the playing field, especially in the area of adequacy and school resources.

The question that seems to burn in everyone's mind is, Does the amount spent on school resources impact student achievement as translated on high-stakes test scores? If it does, then school districts must find innovative ways of dedicating more money toward the allocation of such resources. If it does not, then communities and government bodies should not be concerned whether one district in a state has more or less to spend on its children. However, one thing does not require intensive investigations as to its impact, and that is the impact of a teacher upon his or her students.

For the longest time, teachers have been known to spend much of their own money on resources needed within their classroom. As the summer ends and store circulars are being placed into neighborhood newspapers, teachers frantically search for the best prices on such items as markers, glue sticks, scissors, and notebooks. In some places, teachers have been known to spend up to $500 on various items needed—and not supplied by the district for which they work. From this observation, it seems that teachers understand the connection between materials and retention of knowledge.

While visiting large retail stores in August, one can also observe parents searching for school items found on their child's list. There might even be large boxes decorated with pretty paper, indicating if you are so moved, you might even donate extra school supplies for those children who cannot afford typical purchases. This understanding of the connection between school materials and student achievement is also found among parents and community members. Each person wishes to provide his or her child with all that is necessary to have a successful school year, and if one cannot afford the best, then one attempts to make such sacrifices necessary to do the best that one can do.

Therefore, if school buildings are filled with educators who understand the impact a dollar bill can have on a child's learning experience and parents and community members understand this same fact, then it stands to reason that school boards and superintendents must also see the correlation between spending and test scores. For this reason, one cannot fault a district if it is also attempting to cut back with the end result of having more to give its student population so that each child will have an optimum condition in which to learn and be successful. But what if that is not their reasoning, and support staff numbers are reduced merely as an attempt to gain the community's acceptance, to earn the community's trust as they lay the groundwork for a new proposed bond election? Will the children and teachers still be successful?

> **TIME TO REFLECT**
>
> Do you believe that more supplies are necessary for successful student learning? Does your school district realize the impact of teaching supplies and student learning and seek to provide funding dedicated to the purchasing of such supplies? Or do you, the educator, spend your own money to provide basic classroom supplies? What might a concerned citizen do to engage in a thoughtful discussion with school board members about the need to provide materials to educators so that they may better educate the children?

IMPACT OF CENTRAL OFFICE PERSONNEL

American public education has typically been characterized by periodic swings between centralization and decentralization of power and authority (Cuban 1990; Darling-Hammond 1988; Lindelow & Heynderickx 1989; Mojkowski & Fleming 1988). During times of greater centralized authority, large administrative structures (e.g., states, school districts, and school boards) maintain control over decisions regarding educational policy, budget, and operations. Hence, when the control shifts to the smaller unit (e.g., smaller school boards and individual schools), then decentralization occurs, and those who have the closest connection to the work at hand make the decisions regarding that work.

When a school system, such as the one that Maribeth found herself in, moves to shift some of the power from discipline-specific coordinators back into the classroom, then all roles of its stakeholders (superintendent, other central office personnel, board members, principals, and teachers) are deeply affected. Mutchler (1990) points out, "School-based management and shared decision-making strategies directly challenge and seek to change the complex and well-entrenched patterns of institutional and individual behavior" (p. 4).

According to Ceperley (1991), the role of central office staff members shifts from a primary focus on mandating and monitoring compliance to providing resources and serving as facilitator to those within the school building. Thus the assumption held here is that without those to assist in school-based management and serve as facilitators of change, such as district-specific coordinators, then a successful shift is not likely to occur. There should remain, therefore, a close connection between teachers and central office personnel—especially during periods of change.

Because Maribeth had not had the time to become entrenched in the relational quagmire typical of many central office personnel, she still held tightly to her beliefs in classroom autonomy. She felt that the center of action was found within the classroom and not in the conference room. And because of this, her actions spoke of one serving as facilitator. The institution of a vertical teaming opportunity for those interested in pursuing such a global understanding of the craft was viewed by teachers as a positive step. The creation of a powerful partnership connecting community with content found a valuable opportunity for teachers seeking quality professional development. In direct contrast, the task Maribeth was given at the onset of her central office work—to distribute and monitor usage of the new science curriculum—was seen as negative by all teachers and even some principals. Many new ideas had been tried and proven of worth during Maribeth's short tenure as science coordinator. She could rest in that understanding, even though there were many more still left untested.

> **TIME TO REFLECT**
>
> What are the relationships between central office staff and teachers like in your district? Are they one of support and facilitation, or are they for monitoring and management purposes? What might be done to bring together both groups in an attempt to bridge the divide for the sake of learning?

WHERE TO FROM HERE?

Maribeth sat waiting for the announcement to board a plane for San Francisco. She and a friend were flying west to participate in a science professional development opportunity with the hopes of bringing back to the university something of worth for its preservice and in-service educators. As the call came over the loud speakers, they began to collect their carry-on luggage and make their way to the door. Passengers were unloading and shuffling past on to their next gate. In the midst of the movement, Maribeth spotted the superintendent from the district where she once worked. She felt an intense longing to approach him and say something, but what would be appropriate? The last time Maribeth had spoken to Dr. Monroe was the day of their interview. It seemed such a long time ago, and yet, it had only been 2 years.

Dr. Monroe approached Maribeth, and in that fleeting moment, Maribeth spoke: "Dr. Monroe, thanks for providing me with an opportunity to do something different." He looked at her, probably wondering what stimulated this exchange. Maribeth continued, "Had it not been for the reduction in force, and the loss of a job, I would have never taken the opportunity to move forward, to get my doctor's degree, and to work in a university setting. I would have probably remained with the school district and kept doing what it was that I thought was my dream job. Now I know it was just a stepping stone to something even better." He smiled and walked on. Maribeth smiled, too.

How funny life sometimes is. What we think is a place where we want to remain forever is really a place where we needed to be only a short time to learn the lessons there that will make us ready for something in the future. Yes, there are times when Maribeth remembers fondly the time spent as science coordinator but only for a brief moment in time. There were good times and good friends, but there were also great challenges and perplexing movement within the central office.

Just recently, a friend spoke to Maribeth and announced that once again the central office is hiring even more central office staff members than were there during her tenure. Once again, the pendulum swings. And once again, it is the teachers and students who are caught in its momentum. If decisions are made based solely upon the political whims of powerful groups within the state or community— and decisions seem to be made with each new administrative body taking office—then those who are affected by the changes must find a way to hang on. Teachers and students, even central office personnel, will be swept into in its swift-moving stream. Many will be caught up in the movement; others will simply choose to wait it out.

Yet, the real stake—our children's future—goes on hold once again as we play the game. When will we come to the realization that school buildings were built for the children and that we— teachers and central office personnel—were hired for the children so that they might learn, grow, and develop into the individuals needed for future communities?

REFERENCES

Ceperley, P. (1991). Site-based decision-making: Policymakers can support it or undermine it. *The Link, 10*(1), 7–9.
Cuban, L. (1990). Reforming again, again, and again. *Educational Researcher, 19*(3), 3–13.
Darling-Hammond, L. (1988). Accountability and teacher professionalism. *American Educator, 12*(4), 8–13, 38–43.

Lindelow, J., & Heynderickx, J. (1989). School-based management. In S. C. Smith & P. K. Piele (Eds.), *School leadership: Handbook for excellence* (2nd ed., pp. 104–134). Eugene, OR: ERIC Clearinghouse on Educational Management, College of Education, University of Oregon.

Mojkowski, C., & Fleming, D. (1988). *School-site management: Concepts and approaches*. Andover, MA: Regional Laboratory for Educational Improvement of the Northeast and Islands.

Mutchler, S. E. (1990). Eight barriers to changing traditional behavior: Part one. *Insights on educational policy and practice*. Retrieved July 15, 2008, from http://www.sedl.org/change/issues/issues24.html

10

OPPORTUNITY IN THE FACE OF FAILURE

Sherry Durham

> The Chinese use two brush strokes to write the word 'crisis.' One brush stroke stands for danger; the other for opportunity. In a crisis, be aware of the danger—but recognize the opportunity.
>
> —John F. Kennedy

A PURPOSEFUL CHANGE

Wilson was eager to begin the school year at Valley View Elementary. His years of working in a financial institution had resulted in burnout, and his decision to return to college to receive an education endorsement offered him the chance to find purpose and a new challenge in his life. Teaching a science class to 5th-graders seemed to bring a breath of fresh air into his existence.

To add to his feelings of good fortune, Valley View was known for having high ratings on the accountability tests required by the state and was located in an upscale neighborhood with good parent involvement and strong administrative leadership. Wilson was sure he had made the right choice in accepting this position and making the life-changing decision to become a teacher.

SIGHT UNSEEN

Wilson was about to be faced with an unforeseen glitch in this bright scenario in his life. The leadership at Valley View Elementary was changing. The principal who had been at this campus for several years was being moved to a larger campus in need of improving their accountability scores, and in his place a less experienced individual was taking the leadership role for this campus.

Mr. Johnson was coming from a much smaller school district where he had been the principal at the high school level, much different from Valley View Elementary, which was a 3rd grade through 5th grade campus. Mr. Johnson had ties to the community where Valley View was located and also knew a few of the teachers from his school days.

GUIDING AND LEADING

Guidance is a powerful factor in educational leadership through administration or classroom instructor. The educational leader must guide using control and direction toward new goals that will reinforce the development of a desire to grow and function within a collaborative environment. According to Dewey (1916), "education is . . . a fostering, a nurturing, a cultivating process. All of these words mean that it implies attention to the conditions of growth. . . . Etymologically, the word education means a process of leading or bringing up" (p. 10). Of specific importance is the ability for understanding that sets the tone for learning and leading. Interaction and authenticity allow development of a capacity for knowing.

Dewey (1916) contends, "Of these three words, direction, control, and guidance, the last best conveys the idea of assisting through cooperation" (p. 23). The leaders must use control and direction to maintain focus and reinforce standards of the system, but guidance sets the path for the journey toward learning for students and staff as well. Wilson was in need of guidance in this new environment, and the lack of it made all the difference in his journey.

State accountability testing required students in 5th grade to pass the science test administered in April of each year. The scores on these tests counted toward a campus rating of exemplary, recognized, academically acceptable, or academically unacceptable. Valley View Elementary was known for its standing rating of recognized, which means students are meeting and exceeding the expectations of the state guidelines in areas of math, reading, and science. Banners hanging on the outside of the building advertise the high quality of education offered inside the school's walls, with the dates and ratings proudly displayed largely enough to be seen by passersby from the street.

Students were given the yearly tests in their appropriate grade level, and the results were soon returned to the district. Unfortunately, Valley View Elementary was no longer touted as a state-recognized campus. The scores reflected that 5th-grade science scores were below average, and the school district and campus were shocked that this could have happened on a campus known for its previous high achievement and outstanding instructional practice.

An educational leader must use control and direction to focus and reinforce standards of the learning system. This disciplinary process is described by Foucault (quoted in Anderson and Grinberg 1998) as a "set of discourses, norms, and routines that shape the ways in which . . . educational administration and its related practices (i.e., site-based management, supervision, staff development, etc.) constitute them" (p. 330). When this process breaks down, someone will suffer—either teachers or students. There is always a price to pay when the educational system fails.

On the Valley View campus, the instructional specialist and the principal were looking for answers to why students had not been successful on the 5th-grade science test, which was the targeted area that had kept this campus from being recognized for academic performance. What was different? Was there a change in curriculum? Time on task? Number of students in the classroom? Suddenly a revelation occurred; they recognized that there was a new teacher in this grade level specifically teaching this content area. He must be the reason for the poor scores!

DECIDING FACTORS

Wilson was teaching in a science classroom, but from time to time, he would get off task discussing some current event or a topic relevant to social studies that his students may bring up. He was not included in opportunities to attend district science workshops because the administration believed their campus was covered appropriately with the use of the instructional specialist who offered guidance and updates on all instructional practices for Valley View. When the specialist or principal conducted classroom walk-throughs to assess his performance as an instructor, he rarely received feedback and believed he was doing a good job. The benchmark tests offered data for his students that were not that much different from neighboring campuses in the school district. He was enjoying the students, and other teachers were supportive and welcoming of him to their community of educators. As far as Wilson knew, he was on target with his instructional practice and becoming more secure in his experience at the elementary campus.

The entire campus began to view Wilson as the sole cause for the poor campus rating. Suddenly, there was much discussion re-

> **TIME TO REFLECT**
>
> How do you monitor and assess classroom performance? Have you received appropriate feedback from your administrator, instructional specialist, or mentor?

garding his classroom performance. What had he been teaching? Didn't he have a district scope and sequence of curriculum expectations? Surely he knew what was expected of him in the area of classroom management and the latest science testing requirements! No blame was shared by the campus leadership, even though they had more years of experience in education, the ability to offer professional development to teachers new to content areas, and free access to monitor daily instruction. There was not a minute that the spotlight of detection pointed toward anything they might have neglected to do.

> **TIME TO REFLECT**
>
> How do you view the role of campus administration in the accountability picture for a campus? What amount of influence does a principal have on the test scores of a class? How can he or she offer teachers and students support and motivation for improvement?

When Wilson heard of an opportunity to move to a middle school campus and teach Texas history, he jumped at the chance. The climate of the once-inviting campus had turned into one of isolation and guilt on his part as he truly believed he had made a terrible mistake and wrongly educated children. The campus was as happy to see his exit as he was to make it.

> **TIME TO REFLECT**
>
> How much of the blame belonged to Wilson? What might the district/campus have done to help this first-year teacher?

At his new assignment, Wilson thrived. He had an administrator with a background in curriculum and instruction and a leadership style that included collaborative meetings with staff and allowing the grade levels to meet as teams within the content area to offer her feedback on student progress. The principal or an assistant principal made weekly stops in classrooms to monitor and document strengths or weaknesses observed and shared with the teacher. He was kept updated with the requirements of the state curriculum mandates, involved with professional development in his area of instruction, included in campus planning, and taught how to use student data to drive campus decisions.

> **TIME TO REFLECT**
>
> Does the attitude of the campus administrator toward teachers make a difference in the outcome of testing? Why? How?

In fostering leadership and the development of knowledge, habits must be formed. It is through practice of the administration that these habits become grounded in theory. Foucault (quoted in Anderson and Grinberg 1998) suggests, "In modern society, power is exercised through institutional relations that discipline our way of thinking and acting through self-regulation" (p. 334). Schools must continually focus on ways to improve student achievement. These schools are "most likely to see significant gains as a result of their change efforts" (quoted in Sarason 1996, p. 351).

The difference in the two campuses was not so much a reflection of the attitude or the philosophy of the teacher but that of the administrative team. According to Dufour and Eaker (1998), "teachers ... learn what is important in their schools by observing what is monitored" (p. 108). Dewey (1916) summarizes the role of administration: "In so far as one is interested or concerned in these communications, their matter becomes a part of one's own experience. Active connections with others are such an intimate and vital part of our own concerns that it is impossible to draw sharp lines, such as would enable us to say, 'Here my experience ends, there yours begins'" (p. 186). Regarding the worth of administrative practices, students and teachers will utilize tools they have seen modeled and deemed successful.

Administration can set the standard and provide approaches to leadership that will become common for the good of the learning community. High-stakes tests require high-stakes leadership. This can only be accomplished when leadership is identified as a collaborative process with all stakeholders being active participants in the ongoing process instead of waiting until the results are in and looking for the guilty party. Instead, staff and administration must consistently work together with the focus on assuring students are successful every day, not only on the designated test day in the spring of the year.

REFERENCES

Anderson, G. L., & Grinberg, J. (1998). Educational administration as a disciplinary practice: Appropriating Foucault's view of power, discourse, and method. *Educational Administration Quarterly*, 34(3), 329–353.

Dewey, J. (1916). *Democracy and education: An introduction to the philosophy of education.* New York: Free Press.

Dufour, R., & Eaker, R. (1998). *Professional learning communities at work: Best practices for enhancing student achievement.* Bloomington, IN: National Education Service.

Sarason, S. B. (1996). *Revisiting "the culture of the school and the problem of change."* New York: Teachers College Press.

11

THE CHOICES WE MAKE

Terri Hebert and Sherry Durham

It is our choices . . . that show what we truly are, far more than our abilities.

—J. K. Rowling,
Harry Potter and the Chamber of Secrets

Why teach? This is a question many have attempted to answer through the discourse of educator training. One can be certain it is not for any monetary rewards or fantastic hours, although the misconception still remains among many nonteachers. To help clarify this confusion, teachers do not stroll into their classroom at 8:00 A.M. and leave at 3:00 P.M. with nothing in their hands. Why do you think those nifty rolling carts were made? So teachers wouldn't have back strain carrying the load of papers to grade and books to scour in search of interesting lesson enhancements. And the summer months are not spent lazily relaxing beside a tropical resort with a book in one hand and a cooling drink in another. No, in stark contrast teachers are found at their respective campuses remaining long after the typical school hours—even into the evening preparing for the next day's lesson. Then teachers are expected to return at least 30 minutes prior to the beginning of class to welcome the weary-eyed students back once again.

The corny retorts often shared by teachers about making a difference, touching lives, and creating lifelong learners simply do not do justice to the real reason individuals enter into this profession nor why they choose to stay for many years. It is these men and women who passionately desire to make this world a better place. Yet in order to improve the world, the caliber of people called into teaching must embrace a higher quality with improved life goals while embodying all of the characteristics and abilities necessary to reach all students.

Where do these higher expectations originate? The search for indicative measures that prove high expectations will transfer into even higher results has taken us into the world of politics. NCLB was created from a belief that children would improve their knowledge and skills if there were effective measurements in place. The policy also put forth the notion that teachers could improve their teaching if they were only given documents from which to teach—such as the frameworks or standards. However, we now have confirmed reports that this push toward excellence through standardization has not worked for all. We seem to have gained an understanding throughout our search of data that the "quality of action can never be produced by measurement" (Wheatley 2007, p. 9).

What will invite the problem solvers into the learning experience? How can the creative genius lying dormant inside of children's heads be freed? Oh yes, it is clear now: it is through the standardization of rules and guidelines to be taught so that everyone may be judged against the same criteria regardless of socioeconomics, ethnicity, or learning capability. This will surely offer more depth and breadth of understanding and lead to a generation of thinkers and doers in an effort to improve our society.

Do we really believe this concept? Have we seen it with our own eyes and felt it with our own hearts? Not really. So why do we act as if we believe in the words? Grumet (1988) seeks to capture what this type of learning indicates:

Present is the curriculum, the course of study, the current compliance, general education, computer literacy, master teachers, the liberal arts, reading readiness, time on task. Present is the window. Absent is the ground from which these figures are drawn, negation and aspiration. Absent is the laugh that rises from the belly, the whimper, and the song. Suppressed is the body count, Auschwitz, Bhopal; even the survivors, the hibakusha of Nagasaki and Hiroshima, are invisible. Absent is the darkness and the light. (p. xiii)

As conversations were invited to occur among K–12 teachers across several states, words continue to bring us back to our original thought: All students must be seen as individuals embodying innate strengths and weaknesses that call for more than scripted worksheets and practice pages. Teachers want to be empowered to teach their students! Strategies were discussed, such as using choral readings to assist in building comprehension and further develop vocabulary, yet it echoed of days gone by. There is no need for crayons or colored pencils in today's world of learning unless students are diagramming sentences using color codes for various parts of speech.

Instruction must be timed to the very minute as teachers feel the pressure to move through the content at a frenzied pace. Physical education classes and school lunches are also under careful scrutiny, as state-assisted monitoring promises to ensure healthy and physically fit students. Where does this type of environment leave the classroom teacher? Many report yearning for the day when authentic instruction occurred on a daily basis.

Today's teachers are trained at universities, tested in an attempt to ensure they meet expected standards required for certification, and monitored through an observation process throughout their school tenure. They are required to teach to the state and national standards and, more often than not, given the materials to use within a prescribed time frame in order to offer multiple benchmark tests scheduled throughout the school year. When does the life-changing, creative-thinking, problem-solving instruction happen? Ah yes, it must be found in the stolen moments, the moments that really make a difference, the moments that touch lives and develop a love for learning that will last a lifetime. These are the high-stakes practices that matter.

Don't be confused: Being accountable is a good and necessary tool. All instruction must be of a standard to ensure all students learn what they need to know, but there is much more to the concept than what we have experienced. The conversations presented in this book revealed that good teachers work to first build meaningful relationships with their students. These teachers make it a priority to know the children found in the audience, to talk with parents and guardians while providing assurance of the commitment to excellence. They are confident in their instructional practice and use a variety of learning tools matched with the children.

Standards were used as a framework, but instruction was constantly monitored and adjusted to offer each learner multiple opportunities. There were found a variety of assessments throughout the school year; some were in the formative stages while others were in the summative stage. Portfolios, rubrics, product-based learning, and group presentations were added to engage the learner and involve each learning style. Even high-stakes accountability tests were given, yet they were not the focus of instruction. Teachers spoke of professional development and ongoing trainings as necessary in maintaining their freshness in the classroom and stimulating their interest in their field of expertise. This renewed excitement naturally spilled over into the classroom, inviting learning and hooking the daily lesson to relevant events current to their topics.

What matters most in education today? The recognition of the high stakes of teaching allows educators to meet the required standards but challenges each person to move beyond this narrow existence and reach for student success through the natural use of knowledge and experience to shape learners. The bodies and minds filling today's classrooms will very soon belong to tomorrow's adults, and they will be asked to make decisions about life, welfare, and freedom for the world's population.

It should not be a hope but a certainty that the guidance and instruction offered by the hands of competent, knowledgeable, and caring teachers are enough to shape children into responsible thinkers, creators, and problem solvers for the future good of mankind. High-stakes teaching is founded on a truer path in education not limited by mandated accountability tests and standards where there is one measure for many different learners. Let us not be partners in extinguishing this pursuit, but through good teaching practices, rigorous content, and dedicated efforts, let us use accountability as an added tool instead of the only design for teaching.

REFERENCES

Grumet, M. (1988). *Bitter milk*. Amherst: University of Massachusetts Press.

Wheatley, M. (2007). The uses and abuses of measurement. In L. F. Deretchin & C. J. Craig (Eds.), *International research on the impact of accountability systems: Teacher education yearbook XV* (pp. 7–12). Lanham, MD: Rowman & Littlefield Education.

www.ingramcontent.com/pod-product-compliance
Lightning Source LLC
Chambersburg PA
CBHW021938240426
43668CB00036B/196